W9-AED-720

NO STRINGS

NO STRINGS

A new musical

Book by
SAMUEL TAYLOR

Music and Lyrics by
RICHARD RODGERS

RANDOM HOUSE NEW YORK

Published in New York by Random House, Inc., and simultaneously in Toronto, Canada, by Random House of Canada, Limited.

Photographs by courtesy of Friedman-Abeles

Manufactured in the United States of America

No Strings *was first presented by Richard Rodgers in association with Samuel Taylor at the 54th Street Theatre, New York City, on March 15, 1962, with the following cast:*

(*In order of appearance*)

Barbara Woodruff	Diahann Carroll
David Jordan	Richard Kiley
Jeanette Valmy	Noelle Adam
Luc Delbert	Alvin Epstein
Mollie Plummer	Polly Rowles
Mike Robinson	Don Chastain
Louis de Pourtal	Mitchell Gregg
Comfort O'Connell	Bernice Massi
Gabrielle Bertin	Ann Hodges
First Croupier	Gene Gebauer
Second Croupier	Calvin Von Reinhold
Marcello Agnolotti	Paul Cambeilh

Dancers

Alan Johnson

Susanne Cansino, Julie Drake, Jean Eliot, Ginny Gan, Ellen Graff, Kay Hudson, Ann Hodges, Diana Hrubetz, Sandy Leeds, Anna Marie Moylan, Patti Pappathatos, Janet Paxton, Dellas Rennie, Bea Salten, Carol Sherman, Mary Zahn. Gene Gebauer, Scott Hunter, Larry Merritt, Michael Maurer, David Neuman, Wakefield Poole, Calvin von Reinhold.

MUSICIANS

Flute—Walter Wegner. Clarinet—Aaron Sachs. Oboe—Ernest Mauro. Trumpet—James Sedler. Trombone—James Dahl. Drums—Ronnie Bedford. Bassoon—Walter Kane.

Directed and choreographed by Joe Layton

Settings and lighting by David Hays

Costumes by Fred Voelpel *and* Donald Brooks

Musical direction and dance arrangements by Peter Matz

Orchestrations by Ralph Burns

Associate choreographer: Buddy Schwab

SYNOPSIS

Time: The present

Place: Paris, Monte Carlo,
Honfleur, Deauville, and
St. Tropez

MUSICAL NUMBERS

Prologue

"The Sweetest Sounds"	Barbara and David

Act One

"How Sad"	David
"Loads of Love"	Barbara
"The Man Who Has Everything"	Louis
"Be My Host"	David, Comfort, Mike, Luc, Gabrielle and Dancers
"La La La"	Jeanette and Luc
"You Don't Tell Me"	Barbara
"Love Makes The World Go"	Mollie, Comfort and Dancers
"Nobody Told Me"	David and Barbara

Act Two

"Look No Further"	David and Barbara
"Maine"	David and Barbara
"An Orthodox Fool"	Barbara
"Eager Beaver"	Comfort, Mike and Dancers
"No Strings"	David and Barbara
"Maine"	Barbara and David
"The Sweetest Sounds"	David and Barbara

AUTHORS' NOTE

The part of Barbara Woodruff in *No Strings* is designed to be played by an American colored girl in her early twenties. It is proposed that she also be beautiful, have style, and wear clothes well; be intelligent, witty, warmly human, and wise. The play itself never refers to her color.

Samuel and Richard
thank
Suzanne and Dorothy

PROLOGUE

At rise, the stage is in darkness. A flute is heard. A light appears on a girl standing alone. She is about twenty-four, slim and cool and lovely, with a vibrant spirit and an aliveness you can almost touch. Her name is BARBARA WOODRUFF. *The sound of the flute is augmented; the music has become the introduction to* "The Sweetest Sounds."

BARBARA *(Sings)*

The sweetest sounds I'll ever hear
Are still inside my head.
The kindest words I'll ever know
Are waiting to be said.
The most entrancing sight of all
Is yet for me to see.
And the dearest love in all the world
Is waiting somewhere for me.
Is waiting somewhere, somewhere for me.

(She moves across the stage, and in her light we discover the Musician playing the flute and, standing near him, she sings another chorus of "The Sweetest Sounds." *The Musician wanders off into darkness, playing. The light on the girl blacks out, and she disappears. At the same time, another Musician, playing a clarinet, wanders on at another part of the stage, playing the same theme. Another figure appears. This is a man in his late thirties—tall, lean, full of planes and angles. He moves easily; his eyes are quick and alive. His name is* DAVID JORDAN)

DAVID (*Sings*)

The sweetest sounds I'll ever hear
Are still inside my head.
The kindest words I'll ever know
Are waiting to be said.
The most entrancing sight of all
Is yet for me to see.
And the dearest love in all the world
Is waiting somewhere for me.
Is waiting somewhere, somewhere for me.

(The girl, BARBARA, *reappears in light at another part of the stage, and the Musician with the flute wanders out of darkness to her; and now, facing out, unaware of each other,* BARBARA *and* DAVID *sing another chorus of* "The Sweetest Sounds." *Towards the end of the song, The Musicians move off into darkness, and* BARBARA *and* DAVID *start across the stage. They pass each other, not seeing, unaware, and move off into darkness in different directions, still singing. The song is ended. The stage is dark)*

ACT ONE

ACT ONE

The lights come up on an enormous photographic studio in Paris, and we discover JEANETTE VALMY. JEANETTE *is in her very early twenties, a restless, volatile, swift-moving quintessence of all the young girls of Paris. She is never still, never walks, knows only two ways of progression: dancing and running; and she usually combines the two. The voice of* LUC DELBERT *is heard from off stage.*

LUC Jeanette!

JEANETTE J'arrive!

LUC Apportes-moi le Leica!

JEANETTE Oui, oui, oui.

(She goes racing out. LUC DELBERT *appears. He is a proud young man in his early thirties, dark, brooding, and masculine. He is wheeling a bare clothes model on stage. An ordinary school bell hangs from one of the model's hands. Upstage of him is a long clothes rack filled with hanging dresses, and near the rack are four or five models in various positions. As* LUC *crosses the stage, the bell drops to the floor. The models at the clothes rack come alive)*

LUC No, not yet, girls. I didn't ring the bell.

(The models freeze back into their positions. JEANETTE *comes speeding on, slips a camera over* LUC*'s arm)*

JEANETTE Voilà! (*Without stopping, she speeds to the clothes rack, takes a dress, and runs off stage again*) La robe est magnifique!

LUC (*Calling to her*) Le Rollei! (*The doorbell rings*) Jeanette! On sonne!

JEANETTE (*Speeding on with the camera*) Oui, oui, oui, j'entends!

(*She hands him the camera and races towards the front door. At the same time,* MOLLIE PLUMMER *appears*)

MOLLIE All right! It's open! Jeanette! Slow down! (*She stops* JEANETTE *with outstretched hands*) Some day you're going to go right through a wall. (JEANETTE *laughs.* MOLLIE PLUMMER *is a self-possessed woman of middle years who is an editor of* Vogue. *She combines a happy serenity with a strong executive ability, and she is impressed by no one. She carries a large bag*) Is Barbara here?

LUC Not yet.

MOLLIE Well, so far only normally late.

LUC (*To Jeanette*) Where is the Leica?

JEANETTE Ici!

(*It is around his neck. She races off*)

MOLLIE Luc, why don't you marry the girl and hire a servant?

LUC (*Grins as he checks a camera*) There's not enough work for two.

MOLLIE Yes, she might get bored. You know this is the June cover.

LUC If and when Barbara ever gets here.

MOLLIE It's a disease with that girl. (*She makes herself comfortable, gets a piece of needlepoint out of her bag and starts to work.* LUC *moves the clothes model*) But she claims so many wonderful things happen to you in this world, it's a wonder you ever get where you started to go. It'll be an accident, this time. She'll have seen the most spectacular accident in the Place de la Concorde. (*The doorbell rings*)

LUC (*Calling*) Jeanette! On sonne! (*The school bell drops off the model's hand again, and hits the floor. The models come alive, again*) Not yet, girls! I did not ring the bell!

(*The models freeze, again.* JEANETTE *comes racing on, speeds across the stage and goes off the other side, with* MOLLIE *watching her go*)

MOLLIE I can see another reason why you haven't married her: you can't catch her.

(*A light picks up* DAVID JORDAN *as he appears downstage near the proscenium arch. With him is a bright, handsome, good-humored bum named* MIKE ROBINSON)

DAVID Come on up and see Luc and Jeanette.

MIKE No, I've got a girl waiting and this one I don't keep waiting, not yet. Oh, lovely.

DAVID Where'd you find her?

MIKE I met her in Rome. She was looking for a cup of American coffee, and there I was. I'm giving her the number-one tour.

DAVID Complete?

MIKE With all the trimmings. I showed her the Appian Way and now she wants to app all the time.

JEANETTE (*Off, calling*) Qui est là?

DAVID Jeanette? It's David Jordan!

JEANETTE David! Mais montes! Montes!

DAVID Be there in a minute. (*To* MIKE) Where'll I see you?

MIKE We're having dinner at Moustache. Be there. I told her all about you; she wants to meet the famous author.

DAVID I'll wear my typewriter. What's her name?

MIKE Comfort.

DAVID Ah, come on.

MIKE David, I swear! Comfort O'Connell from Tulsa, Oklahoma. And rich!

DAVID And pretty?

MIKE Pretty! She's got the most beautiful letter of credit you ever saw in your life.

DAVID You look all set for the winter.

MIKE Knock on wood, knock on wood! (*He starts off fast, then stops short*) Hey! We're going to Monte Carlo at the end of the week for the auto races. Want to come?

DAVID Who pays?

MIKE She pays! Who else?

DAVID You're on. See you later.

MIKE Comfort! I come!
(*He races off.* DAVID *grins and enters the studio*)

DAVID (*Calls*) Jeanette! Luc!
(*They come racing to him, and* JEANETTE *throws herself into his arms*)

JEANETTE David! David!

DAVID Hey, Jeanette!

LUC Jeanette, that's enough. (*He is pulling Jeanette off*) Jeanette! It's enough, I say! (*He pulls* JEANETTE *off* DAVID, *then almost leaps upon him with joy*) David!

DAVID Hello, my old.
(*They shake hands vigorously*)

LUC But how marvelous! Where have you been? How long is it? Months!

DAVID Almost a year.

LUC Why? What have you been doing?

DAVID Knocking around. Spain, mostly. Then over to Rome. Then back to Madrid.

LUC But now you'll stay in Paris for a while.

DAVID Yes, I'm hungry for Paris.

JEANETTE And Paris is hungry for you!

DAVID How do you like that, Luc? And in English, yet!
(JEANETTE *laughs happily*)

LUC David Jordan, Mollie Plummer.

MOLLIE How do you do.

DAVID How do you do.

LUC Miss Plummer is an editor of *Vogue*.
(DAVID *looks again*)

MOLLIE (*Placidly*) I know what you're thinking.

DAVID (*Politely*) Oh, not at all.

MOLLIE Not at all what?

DAVID Whatever you think I was thinking. I like that.

MOLLIE You should, it's Balenciaga. It just doesn't look very Balenciaga on me. Sometimes I look in the mirror and say: "Physician, heal thyself." And then I think, what for? I'm comfortable.

DAVID I'm devoted to *Vogue*.

MOLLIE How nice of you to say so.

DAVID I read it religiously.

MOLLIE It's the only way to read it.

DAVID But you're not French.

MOLLIE That's right.

DAVID And still, an editor of Paris *Vogue.*

MOLLIE I took French in high school.

DAVID (*Agreeing*) Ah, well! Then maybe you can answer a question for me. Do women dress for men, or for other women?

MOLLIE I'll give you the short answer: men.

DAVID Poor things. What a waste.

MOLLIE You mean you feel sorry for women?

DAVID Why not? They're missing out on the most wonderful thing in the world.

MOLLIE What?

DAVID Women. (*He sings* "How Sad")

What are the poor girls getting?
To whom do they raise a voice?
What are the poor girls netting?
They just have Hobson's choice.
They crane their delicate necks
But there's just one opposite sex.

(*Refrain*)
How sad—to be a woman.
Women are stuck with men.
A lady's life must be dreary
Without a lady to call "Dearie."
A woman's cheek is for caressing.

A man's is trouble;
It's mostly stubble.
It's sad—and so depressing.
Ladies, I ask again:
How can a woman
Be like a woman?
What do they see in men?

A woman's hand is tiny;
A man has just a paw.
A woman's mouth is soft and sweet;
A man has just a jaw.
Beneath her chin lies Heaven,
While under his is hair.
In fact, she's entirely Heaven;
It's blissful to be there.
How can they make such a fuss
Over ugly, sinful, predatory
Bums like us!

(DAVID *picks up the school bell and rings it, and immediately the models at the clothes rack come alive, and other models start moving on stage from the wings*)

LUC No, girls! I didn't ring the bell! David, please don't ring the bell! (*He starts to shoo the models off stage again*) No! Go! Back to your dressing rooms! I don't need you, yet! Go! (*But* DAVID *continues to ring the bell, and the music continues to play; and in spite of* LUC'S *frantic efforts, the stage is soon filled with girls moving, dancing, whirling by, as* DAVID *happily watches them.* LUC *retrieves the bell from* DAVID. DAVID *sings another chorus of* "How Sad," *the song ends, and the girls come to a stop.* LUC *gazes at them wearily*) Not yet, girls. I didn't ring the bell.

(*The girls all troop back to their dressing rooms*)

DAVID Luc? What are we shooting today?

LUC A cover. If you will stop fooling around and my model ever arrives.

DAVID Who's the model? Angélique?

JEANETTE (*Derisively*) Ho! Angélique!

LUC Angélique has married a fake Italian Count—and now lives in Bologna—

JEANETTE —et elle a beaucoup grossi! Comme ça!

BARBARA (*Off*) I'm here!

JEANETTE Baba!

(*She starts to speed out, but* BARBARA *meets her coming in and takes her in her arms*)

BARBARA Hello, my pet. Mollie, I'm late.

MOLLIE Oh, no!

(BARBARA *bends down and kisses her on the cheek*)

BARBARA Don't be angry, my darling. I just wish you could have seen the accident in the—

MOLLIE (*Finishing it*) —Place de la Concorde.

BARBARA (*Wide-eyed*) No, the Place de l'Alma! And Mollie, you never saw anything like it! Luc, are you waiting for me?

LUC Evidently.

(*During all of the following, which she tells with great enthusiasm,* BARBARA *takes off her coat, takes the scarf off her head, hands things to* JEANETTE, *who is busily waiting on her, kicks off her shoes, gets* JEANETTE *to unzip her dress, and starts to get out of it before she disappears into the other room to change*)

BARBARA There were taxis scattered all over the Place! And one went right up into a sidewalk cafe . . . and all the gendarmes running about blowing their whistles—what color shoes?

MOLLIE The green. But you weren't in a taxi.

BARBARA No, I had Louis' car and driver. But I had to stop and see! And oh, Mollie, the traffic was backed up all the way to the Champs Elysées, and across the bridge to the Left Bank—please help me, Jeanette. And the taxi drivers all out on the street screaming at each other . . . oh, Mollie, I learned the most beautiful new words!

(*And she is gone,* JEANETTE *with her*)

MOLLIE Well then, the afternoon wasn't totally lost.

BARBARA (*Off*) Mollie, you don't believe me! Have you never seen an accident in Paris?

MOLLIE Well, I've seen taxis hit each other, but in Paris that's not an accident, it's a way of life.

(BARBARA *laughs gleefully*)

DAVID Luc, who is she?

LUC The most marvelous model! Eh, Mollie?

MOLLIE I think so, yes.

LUC So alive, I never want to stop shooting her. Her name is Barbara Woodruff; she is called Baba.

DAVID An American?

LUC Yes, Mollie discovered her, and trained her.

MOLLIE What part of America are you from?

DAVID New England.
(JEANETTE *comes back and goes to* DAVID)

LUC David is a writer, you know. A fine writer!

MOLLIE Oh!

LUC What were you doing in Madrid, David? Writing?

DAVID The additional dialogue for an Italian movie.

MOLLIE Oh?

JEANETTE Who was the star? Sophia Loren? Lollobrigida?

DAVID Somebody new, honey, sort of a cross between the two. Long face, short body. She played the Whore of Babylon.

MOLLIE Oh, a religious picture.

DAVID Could we have a scoop? Make it cognac.
(JEANETTE *dashes out*)

LUC (*Defending him*) But you have been writing for yourself, David, eh? Your novel! What of the novel you started last summer in Biarritz?
(JEANETTE *brings* DAVID *a bottle of cognac and a glass*)

DAVID I threw that away. But yes, I did start another. I ditched everybody for a while, and got off to Switzerland, and started to write. Then your pals found me.

JEANETTE But, David, what about the novel you started in St. Tropez?

DAVID (*Wryly*) No, that was the summer before last. I forget what happened to that one. Luc, I bumped into Mike Robinson; we're going down to Monte Carlo for the races. You coming?

LUC Yes, I have to take pictures for Mollie. These days we shoot high fashion everywhere.

BARBARA (*Off*) Luc?

LUC Yes?

BARBARA Who's your visitor?

LUC David Jordan!

MOLLIE He's an American, dear.

BARBARA Oh. Tourist?

LUC No, he is an old friend. He has lived in Europe for many years.

BARBARA (*Off*) Oh! One of those. Escaping taxes?

LUC He has no taxes to escape.

DAVID Explain that I am poor but honest, Luc.

MOLLIE Now, there's a phrase I never could understand. Poor but honest. Why don't they ever say rich but honest? If you're poor, it's almost a cinch you're honest.

(BARBARA *sweeps on wearing a beautiful, floating dress; and she looks wonderful*)

LUC Barbara Woodruff, David Jordan.

DAVID How do you do?

(BARBARA *sweeps past him, seeming barely to notice him*)

BARBARA Hello. Mollie, is it all right?

MOLLIE Yes, it's lovely, dear. Up you go.

(*She shoos* BARBARA *towards the posing platform*)

LUC Jeanette, the fan.

(JEANETTE *gets a fan and plugs it in.* BARBARA *gets into place*)

BARBARA (*As she goes*) What'll you have, Luc?

LUC Everything.

BARBARA The bit. The whole, lovely bit. (*The fan blows her dress*) Ah, heaven, Jeanette. Here we go.

(*She stamps on the floor three times in imitation of the rise of a theatre curtain in France, then strikes a pose*)

LUC Good. (*He clicks the camera. From now on,* BARBARA *strikes a series of poses that are reminiscent of and almost caricatures of every pose of every model ever seen in* Vogue. *Now she strides, now she straddles; an arm goes up, an arm goes out; the head is back, then tilted; the back is arched, and then she slopes forward, round-shouldered; now she is surprised, now tantalizing, now laughing, now coolly demure, now bitchy, now disdainful, now hopelessly appealing. And all the while,* LUC *is snapping cameras, sometimes using the one fixed on the tripod, more often moving about and clicking with the cameras slung around his neck, forever making noises of approval and disapproval, and sometimes giving orders to* BARBARA *and* JEANETTE) Yes. (*Click*) . . . yes. (*Click*) . . . no . . . no . . . (*Click*) Marvelous! (*Click*)

BARBARA (*Intent on her work*) What does your American do, Luc?

LUC He's a writer.
(*Click*)

BARBARA What does he write?

MOLLIE He starts novels.

BARBARA Who finishes them?

JEANETTE Mais non, Baba! He is a great writer, David. Hein, Luc?

LUC Bien sûr, he has won a great prize. Enough of the fan. (JEANETTE *unplugs the fan and puts it away*) Baba, give me the mouths, now, all the mouths. (*He moves to a new position*) It had a name. David, tell them the name of the prize you have won.
(DAVID *goes on drinking*)

BARBARA (*As she goes on posing*) Mollie knows everything. Mollie, what did he win?

MOLLIE (*Intent on her needlework*) Who?

BARBARA David Jordan.

MOLLIE The Victoria Cross?
(BARBARA *keeps changing poses*)

BARBARA Do they give that for writing novels?

MOLLIE They ought to give it for reading some.

BARBARA Maybe he got it for finishing one.
(DAVID *gently puts down the bottle and the glass*)

DAVID I'll see you later, Luc.

JEANETTE Mais non, David, ne pars pas! Baba!

BARBARA Mmmm?

MOLLIE (*Placidly*) I'm afraid we've hurt his feelings, dear.

BARBARA (*Regretfully*) Ohhh!

DAVID (*To* LUC) See you at Moustache for dinner. I'll be with Mike Robinson and a new friend.

LUC Wait, David, I'm almost finished.

BARBARA Mr. Jordan! That's enough, Luc. I've run out of mouths. (*She comes down to* DAVID, *and is all sincerity and charm*) I'm terribly sorry, and I'm sure Jeanette's right; you're probably enormously famous, but Mollie and I wouldn't know. She still hasn't finished reading *Anthony Adverse,* and I read nothing but spicy French novels, so you see! Someone could walk in who'd won the Pulitzer Prize, and we wouldn't know the difference.

JEANETTE Pulitzer! Mais c'est ça!

LUC Yes, that's it. The Pulitzer Prize. I knew it was a name.
(BARBARA *looks at* MOLLIE, *who shrugs. She looks back at* DAVID, *who has regarded her steadfastly*)

BARBARA (*Sweetly*) How nice. I . . . don't suppose you'd know the title.

LUC This I do remember! *Plan of Attack!*

JEANETTE Oui, c'est ça! *Plan of Attack!* Et c'était publié ici en France, et dans tous les pays du monde!
(*She moves off into darkness*)

BARBARA All over the world.

DAVID It's all right, it was before your time.

BARBARA I do read.
(LUC *disappears.* DAVID *moves across to* BARBARA. *The darkness closes in*)

DAVID What have you got against Americans?

BARBARA Some of my best friends are Americans.

DAVID Will you come have a drink?

BARBARA I don't drink.
(*They regard each other without expression*)

DAVID I'll walk you home.

BARBARA I've a car waiting.

DAVID Send him away.

BARBARA It's a long walk home.

DAVID It's a nice day.
(A pause. The darkness is closing in, and MOLLIE *is barely seen)*

BARBARA Mollie, do you need me?

MOLLIE No, dear.

BARBARA Would you like Louis' car and driver to take you back to the office?

MOLLIE Yes, I would.
(She rises, takes her bag)

BARBARA Will you tell him I won't need him any more today?

MOLLIE Yes, I will.
(She walks off into the darkness. The light has closed in on DAVID *and* BARBARA. *A pause)*

BARBARA I'll go change.
(She walks off into darkness; he watches her go. Musicians appear, playing. Scenery begins to fall into place; we are now on a Paris street. Figures appear, and move along the street. Call them people of Paris, but they are without identity, and they move with a rhythm of their own. As the scenery changes, and the people move by, DAVID *looks off after* BARBARA*)*

DAVID (*Sings* "The Sweetest Sounds")
What's real?
She's real.
I'm real, too.
Everything about us shifts and changes,
Only we are real.

(*Refrain*)
The sweetest sounds I'll ever hear
Are still inside my head.
The kindest words I'll ever know
Are waiting to be said.
The most entrancing sight of all
Is yet for me to see.
And the dearest love in all the world
Is waiting somewhere for me.
Is waiting somewhere, somewhere for me.

(BARBARA *appears. She is dressed as we first saw her, but she does not wear the scarf on her head. She stops before* DAVID *and smiles*)

BARBARA All right?

DAVID Where do you live?

BARBARA That way.

DAVID Left Bank?

BARBARA (*Nods*) Just off the Champs de Mars. The Eiffel Tower stands outside my window.

DAVID How very Parisian.

BARBARA Oh, yes. I work at being Parisian. (*With a bright smile*) I'm sorry about your book. Were we very rude?

DAVID Yes, you were. Are you always that way when you first meet fellow Americans?

BARBARA I think so, it's not meant to be rudeness. It's a kind of wariness, a kind of fending off, I guess.

DAVID (*Gently*) There's no need of wariness. You don't have to fend me off.

(*A moment as they look at each other, and then she looks away almost shyly. And then*)

BARBARA (*Bright again*) Why haven't we met before, if you're such a good friend of Luc's?

DAVID I've been out of Paris.

BARBARA How long?

DAVID Close to a year. You probably weren't here, then.

BARBARA Oh, yes. But I was still just a little girl trying.

DAVID And now you've made it. And big. (*She smiles*) The cover of *Vogue,* and a car and a driver. (*A moment*) Who is Louis?

BARBARA (*Smiling nicely*) You wanted to walk. (*A moment, then they start and move into the scene. As they do, the Musicians wander off, and the music stops, and the passing figures fade away*) Tell me about the book. It was called *Plan of Attack* and won the Pulitzer Prize, and I don't know it. Is it a war book? (*He nods*) But you must have been terribly young!

DAVID A baby.

BARBARA Did you enlist as a drummer boy?

DAVID I was wounded at the Battle of Bull Run. (*She laughs*)

BARBARA But you *were* young.

DAVID I waited awhile to write it.

BARBARA When was it published?

DAVID Eight years ago.

BARBARA Did you write it here?

DAVID Back home.

BARBARA Where is home?

DAVID Bear Isle, Maine.

BARBARA (*Her imagination stirred*) Bear Isle, Maine! You lived on an island off the coast of Maine! Ah, no, it's too romantic, you're making it up. (*He grins*) Truly the rock-bound coast of Maine? And is it really rock-bound and grim and forbidding?

DAVID And gentle and caressing.

BARBARA And what do the people do?

DAVID My father was a quarryman—he cut granite. My uncles were lobstermen. My mother was a schoolteacher.

BARBARA And did you learn to cut granite and fish lobsters?

DAVID Oh, yes.

BARBARA It sounds like the most romantic place in the world. How could you bear to leave it?

DAVID For Paris?

BARBARA Oh. Yes. You can leave anything for Paris.

DAVID You too.

BARBARA I didn't leave much. And so now Paris is home for you too.

DAVID Paris . . . Rome . . . Switzerland . . . two homes have I: the world and Paris.

BARBARA And what have you written since then? Since your book?

DAVID Not very much.

BARBARA What was that joke about starting novels?
(*Pause.* DAVID *stares straight ahead*)

DAVID (*Grimly*) I start novels. (*She looks up at him curiously. They wander on. A piece of scenery drops in and screens them from sight as they walk, and scenery rises, and more scenery drops in, and we are in another part of Paris, and musicians wander on, playing, and the anonymous figures appear, and move along the street, and the rhythm is heightened.* DAVID *and* BARBARA *stroll on from another direction, in silence. During the following, the Musicians wander off, the music fades out, the passing figures disappear*) You're sure you wouldn't like to stop and have a drink.

BARBARA I honestly don't drink. But we can stop, if you'd like. (*He is looking about. None of the scenery shows a café*) You had quite a bit of brandy at Luc's.

DAVID (*Coldly*) Oh? By whose standards?

(BARBARA *is caught, and is chagrined and amused*)

BARBARA So sorry. There's a little place just over there. . . .

DAVID No, never mind.

BARBARA Oh, do let's stop. I'll have a lemonade.

DAVID No. Forget it.

BARBARA But I'd love a citron pressé! I didn't mean to imply you're a drunkard.

DAVID We'll both have a citron pressé.

BARBARA Don't be silly. If you want a brandy, of course you'll have a brandy.

(*She starts off; he stops her*)

DAVID (*With good humor*) We're having our first quarrel. (*And she laughs, but then looks up at him and scans his face seriously. After a moment*) What is it? (*The Musicians and passing figures are gone; the music has stopped*)

BARBARA Why did you ask me?

DAVID What?

BARBARA To come for a drink, to go for a walk?

DAVID I don't know yet. A beautiful girl was deliberately rude—

BARBARA Aren't you curious?

DAVID Yes.

BARBARA I've asked you a hundred questions; you haven't asked me one.

DAVID I have time, I think . . . haven't I? (*A moment*) What would you like to tell me?

BARBARA What would you like to know?

DAVID What's your name?

BARBARA Barbara Woodruff.

DAVID Where were you born?

BARBARA New York City.

DAVID Where did you live?

BARBARA Uptown. Way uptown.

DAVID Where did you go to school?

BARBARA George Washington High.

DAVID That's enough for one time, don't you think? (*She nods*) One more question. (*She waits*) What do you want?

BARBARA The world.

DAVID What will you settle for?

BARBARA The world.

DAVID How would you like it wrapped?

BARBARA In pink and gold with a big blue ribbon.

DAVID Does it ever come wrapped that way?

BARBARA Mine will. If it doesn't, I'll take it back and exchange it for another world! (*She sings* "Loads of Love")

I never have been handed much,
I never have demanded much.
I just want money,
A nice position,
And loads of lovely love.
I never have expected much,
I never have rejected much.
I want my dinner,
Some conversation,
And loads of lovely love.

The dumb ones go for quantity,
The wise ones go for quality.
I've got the answer now:
It's not how much—it's how!

I do not ask for bliss, I guess.
It all boils down to this, I guess:
I just want money,
And then some money,
And loads of lovely love!

My work fulfills me,
It never kills me.
So far I'm not a wife, so
I organize my life so
No one annoys me,
No one enjoys me
Unless we're equal partners in the fun.
Through the week I work and play and give.
Even on Sunday, I love to live!

(*Refrain*)
I never have been handed much,
I never have demanded much.
I just want money,
A nice position,
And loads of lovely love.
I never have expected much,
I never have rejected much.
I want my dinner,
Some conversation,
And loads of lovely love.
A bud appears and then it's May,
So first things first, I always say.
The horse precedes the cart.
It isn't heft, it's heart!
I do not ask for bliss, I guess.
It all boils down this, I guess:
I just want money,
And then some money,
And loads of lovely love!

(*They start walking again, the music continues to play, scenery moves, scenery drops into place, Musicians and figures flow through. We are in another part of Paris, and* BARBARA *whirls about and picks up the song again with the music.* DAVID *buys a bunch of violets from a street vendor*)

I never have been pampered much,
I never have been hampered much.
I just want money,
A nice position,
And loads of lovely love.
I do not ask for bliss, I guess.
It all boils down to this, I guess:
I just want money,
And then some money,
And loads of lovely love!

(*The song is ended.* DAVID *puts the bunch of violets in her hand.* BARBARA *turns to* DAVID *and smiles*) I'm home.

DAVID Over there?

BARBARA (*Nods and points*) You see? The Eiffel Tower really does sit in my back yard.

DAVID It must be rather frightening to live with, close to.

BARBARA Oh no, I love it. And I never have to wonder where I am when I wake up in the morning.

DAVID You're lucky; I often do. May I come up?

BARBARA No. (*She takes her bag from him*) Thank you. Goodbye.

DAVID Will I see you again?

BARBARA I should think so. It seems we travel in the same set: the Paris Whiz Kids.

DAVID I'll call you tomorrow.

BARBARA I'd rather you didn't.

DAVID Why? (*No answer*) Do you have what the French so delicately call "a friend"?

BARBARA (*Gently*) Did you decide it was your turn to be rude? (*She grins*) Thank you for the walk and the violets. (*She walks away and out of sight.* DAVID *turns and wanders off into the crowd, and we are in* BARBARA'S *apartment. Seated there is a man, sipping champagne, with the bottle in a cooler at his side. He is beautifully groomed, impeccably dressed; he is quietly reserved but very much alive; he has humor and an ironic view of the world. He is in his fifties. His name is* LOUIS DE POURTAL. BARBARA, *from off stage*) Louis, are you here?

LOUIS Yes, I'm here.

BARBARA (*Entering*) I'm sorry I'm late. Where are we dining tonight? Somewhere dressy?

LOUIS I thought perhaps in the garden at Laurent—

BARBARA Oh, good! Very dressy!

LOUIS —if you don't think you'll be cold.

BARBARA I'm never cold when I'm chic. What is the champagne? Something you brought? Or did I have it here?

LOUIS I brought it. (*He offers the glass*) Come. Try it.

BARBARA No, thanks.

LOUIS (*Firmly*) Come. You will tell me the name and tell me the year.

BARBARA Ah, Louis, why must I always be tested! I don't even like the stuff.

LOUIS Come, come. It is part of your education. (*She sips the wine, and considers, then gives her judgment*)

BARBARA Napa Valley, California, 1898. (LOUIS *laughs*) But no, Louis, I am getting better, admit it.

LOUIS Yes, you are.

BARBARA And I am a good pupil.

LOUIS You're a very good pupil.

BARBARA Last night I guessed the wine you were drinking.

LOUIS You guessed it was red.

BARBARA Ah, no, Louis, you're making fun of me, and I really did guess it. You wait and see: tonight at Laurent I'll taste all your wines, and I'll guess every one of them.

LOUIS (*Chuckling contentedly*) We'll see. And now, my star pupil, will you change for dinner?

BARBARA (*Brightly*) Okay.

(*She starts out, but then stops short as she thinks of* DAVID; *and he appears at one side of the stage, in her mind*)

DAVID I'll call you tomorrow.

BARBARA I'd rather you didn't.

LOUIS (*Placidly*) Did you have a good walk?

(*Which brings* BARBARA *sharply out of her reverie. She glances at* LOUIS *quickly*)

BARBARA Yes.

(*She starts out again*)

LOUIS What is his name, the tall American?

(BARBARA *stops short again, then turns on* LOUIS *with a great smile of despair and amusement*)

BARBARA Oh, Louis, I wish you wouldn't have that driver of yours spy on me so. Here, unhook the top.

(*She kneels on the floor with her back to him*)

DAVID Do you have what the French so delicately call "a friend"?

BARBARA (*In reverie*) Did you decide it was your turn to be rude?

LOUIS It is not a matter of being rude, my treasure. One happens to have someone who accidentally observes.

BARBARA Well, I can't go anywhere without that driver being accidentally around. Do you know, the other day he tried to follow me into the ladies' room at the Ritz?

LOUIS I will tell him to be less intrusive.

BARBARA Or at least teach him to read. Why do you do that, Louis?

LOUIS What?

BARBARA Have me watched? Since you're not my lover?

LOUIS It is because I am not your lover.

BARBARA And you want to be sure there's nobody else? There's nobody else.

LOUIS And you do have everything you want.

BARBARA Everything . . .

DAVID What's your name?

BARBARA Barbara Woodruff

LOUIS A car . . .
a chauffeur . . .
a beautiful apartment . . .

DAVID What do you want?

BARBARA The world.

LOUIS . . . everything!

BARBARA *comes out of her reverie and smiles at him*)

BARBARA I don't think anyone could give me everything I want, Louis. (DAVID *drifts off into darkness*) But you do make a good try. And you are a patient man.

LOUIS So far.

BARBARA (*With a rueful smile*) Ah, Louis, are you getting impatient? I'm sorry, really I am. But we're not in love, and when you're not in love you don't fall into being a mistress that easily. At least I don't. Do you want to call it off?

LOUIS No. A bargain's a bargain. I can wait. For the time being, you are the ornament on my arm, the loveliest ornament in Paris. And for the time being, that will have to do.

BARBARA (*With a wicked grin*) Well, I think it's a very classy arrangement. (*She moves up to the bedroom door*) I wish the girls at George Washington High could just see me now!

LOUIS Barbara, do you think you will love me?

BARBARA (*Honestly*) I hope so.

(*She goes. Four Musicians at another part of the stage, seated as a quartet, begin to play*)

LOUIS (*Sings* "The Man Who Has Everything")

The man who has everything is wealthy.
He goes where he wants to and when.
The man who has everything is healthy, too,
So he can run around from midnight to ten.
The girl whom I've chosen for my quarry
Is dressed by Chanel or by Dior;
Behind the wheel of my Ferrari
I can ask for anything more.
The man who has everything has nothing
Till love all his own he can see.
I think it may be true
It never will be you
But meanwhile I have everything; lucky me!

My paintings are Pollacks and Picassos.
They hang so terribly straight.
My silver is hallmarked, my glass is Baccarat

I have service for forty-and-eight
(People).
My chiropodist visits me weekly.
(I hate bending over, you see.)
The clothes that fit me so sleekly
Are a passionate pleasure to me.
In truth I really represent
The nearly complete gentleman.

(*Refrain*)
The man who has everything is wealthy.
He goes where he wants to and when.
The man who has everything is healthy, too,
So he can run around from midnight to ten.
I fly off to Switzerland for skiing,
But sit on the terrace sipping Scotch.
I'm just a seeing human being,
If I can't do something I watch!
The man who has everything has nothing
Till love all his own he can see.
I think it will be true
It never will be you
But meanwhile I have everything; lucky me!
Lucky me!

(BARBARA *re-enters towards the end of the song, dressed in a housecoat, and watches him. At the end of the song, she goes to him and kisses him gently on the cheek*)

BARBARA Lucky me.

LOUIS You still haven't told me his name.

BARBARA Who?

LOUIS The interested American.

(DAVID *re-appears at another part of the stage*)

BARBARA Oh. David Jordan. He's not interested, darling; only intrigued. I met him at Luc's.

DAVID Will I see you again?

BARBARA (*In space*) Why haven't we met before?

LOUIS David Jordan? He's been out of Paris for about a year.

BARBARA Do you know him?

LOUIS Yes. Always in Europe there is one American everyone knows. Strange, it is almost always a writer.

DAVID I want to see you again.

BARBARA Does he write well?

LOUIS (*Shrugs*) Who can tell? Since he no longer writes. Once he wrote well. Americans are always so full of promise....

BARBARA What does he do now?

LOUIS He is a "Europe bum." Do you know what that is? (*She shakes her head*) You've heard of "tennis bums" . . . and "ski bums" . . .

BARBARA Oh, yes.

LOUIS Well, this one is a "Europe bum."

BARBARA What does he do?

LOUIS Wanders around Europe.

BARBARA But doing what?

LOUIS Whatever he can to stay in Europe. He writes cheap Italian films; sometimes he acts in them. He flies planes for money; he's a good pilot, I've used him myself. He skis well, he swims well, he sails boats, he plays tennis well. He is invited to the best houses in the most popular places in Europe. Everyone knows him; he is everyone's friend. And so he lives.

BARBARA How awful!

LOUIS There are some Americans that Europe destroys.

BARBARA Not this American.
(*She steps into the bedroom for a moment, and comes back with two dinner dresses*)

LOUIS And then there are some Americans who have to come to Europe to be born.

BARBARA You're so right; that's me. (*She holds up the dresses*) Which one? Celle-ci, ou celle-là?

LOUIS Ni celle-ci, ni celle-là. I'll find what I want.
(*He starts off*)

DAVID How very Parisian.

BARBARA Oh, I work at being Parisian.

LOUIS (*As he moves out*) Yes, you do. You are a very good pupil.

(*He is gone, and* BARBARA *and* DAVID *are left alone. The darkness closes in on them until the background is gone and they are alone in separate light*)

BARBARA Where is home?

DAVID Bear Isle, Maine.

BARBARA Is it really rock-bound and grim and forbidding?

DAVID (*Wandering off*) And gentle and caressing.

BARBARA How could you bear to leave it?

DAVID For Paris? For Europe?

(*He is gone. She stands thinking for a moment, then turns away and disappears. We hear a trumpet, there is movement and light, and we are in Monte Carlo. The auto races are on; we see people watching.* MIKE ROBINSON *appears, calling*)

MIKE Comfort! Comfort! (DAVID *appears below, carrying a small leather portable bar*) Hey, David, where's my girl?

DAVID How would I know? I'm looking for one of my own.

COMFORT (*Calling*) Hey, where are my men?

(*A bright, fresh, driving American girl in her late twenties comes speeding onto the scene. This is* COMFORT O'CONNELL. *She has a bottle of Coca Cola in her hand*)

DAVID Oh, there she is! Hi, Comfort.

COMFORT Hi, David. David, how much is a hundred francs in American money?

DAVID About twenty dollars.

COMFORT Twenty dollars for a Coca Cola!

MIKE Comfort, what happened to you?

COMFORT Oh, I just decided to take off early.
(MIKE *puts a proprietary arm around her, and kisses her*)

MIKE You had me worried, honey. I woke up and looked around—

COMFORT I decided to be a real tourist. Hey, this Monte Carlo! I went to the Casino and dropped a bundle—

DAVID In the morning?

COMFORT Well, just sort of a breakfast bundle. Then I went up the hill to see the castle where Grace Kelly lives, and then I found a bookstore and bought a dirty book. Look! *The Forty-seven*—

MIKE (*Taking it*) Comfort, you don't need that.

COMFORT Oh, I don't know. There's one about a donkey and two baskets—

MIKE Honey, we're plain, simple people.

COMFORT It looked kind of interesting. You know, I think I'll buy a couple of hundred copies of that and send it to my friends back home. It could revolutionize Tulsa. How long does this auto race last?

DAVID Oh, about another hour.

COMFORT And the cars go right through the streets! What a cockeyed beautiful place to live in! Mike, a drink!

(MIKE *opens the portable bar and makes drinks for them all*)

DAVID (*Sees* LUC *off stage*) Hey, Luc! Comfort, there's someone for you to know. Luc Delbert: the best photographer in Paris.

COMFORT Does he need a job? My old man owns a piece of *Look*, or *Life*, or something.

MIKE Honey, he works for *Vogue*. And for practically everybody else.

(LUC *strolls in with a striking-looking French girl with long black hair and a sullen expression. Luc wears his jacket draped over his shoulders, the sleeves dangling*)

DAVID Hey, Luc!

COMFORT Who's the girl?

MIKE Gabrielle Bertin, the singer. She gets around too.

LUC David!

(*They shake hands enthusiastically*)

DAVID Luc, do you know Comfort O'Connell? Luc Delbert—and this is Gabrielle Bertin.

COMFORT Pleased to meet you.

LUC I am charmed.

COMFORT And if you ever need a job, call me. (*She takes a look at* GABRIELLE *and her mouth drops open with amazed recognition. To* GABRIELLE) Hey, I know you! I've got all your records! Those great songs about LIFE! (*She does a quick, four-bar imitation of Piaf*) Oh, you're great!

(*She crosses to get her drink, and* GABRIELLE *and* MIKE *follow her*)

DAVID Luc, is that model down here with you? The one I met at your studio? Barbara Woodruff?

LUC Barbara? No, she is in Paris. Why?

DAVID I kept calling her, I couldn't get her.

MIKE Hey, Luc, this is Comfort's first trip to Europe.

LUC Oh! Then we must show you everything, eh? Have you been to Paris?

COMFORT Have I been to Paris? Mike, tell him about me and Paris!

MIKE Well, it's still standing. But she only had four days.

LUC But you are going back.

COMFORT And how!

LUC Then I will give you a party.

Polly Rowles, Richard Kiley, Noelle Adam, and Alvin Epstein
as MOLLIE PLUMMER, DAVID JORDAN, JEANETTE VALMY,
and LUC DELBERT

MIKE Luc, will you do that? In your studio? Hey, David!

DAVID That's a great idea. Comfort, he throws the best parties in Paris.

COMFORT Done and done! On one condition. I buy the champagne.

LUC Done.

COMFORT It's a deal. I want to learn all about Paris: where you go, what you do, who you talk to—

LUC Oh, that is more complicated than you think. There are people who have lived in Paris all their life who still do not know.

COMFORT Oh, I'm a quick learner.

LUC For instance, the places to go: you must never be found on the Right Bank after dark.

COMFORT Never?

DAVID Never.

COMFORT (*To* MIKE) But we stayed at the Ritz! That's on the Right Bank.

GABRIELLE Oh, for going to bed, the Ritz is lovely!

COMFORT You found that out too.

LUC Another example. Here in Monte Carlo. You never go up on the hill to look at the castle. That is for tourists.

COMFORT I did it, and I'm glad.

LUC Do you like Monte Carlo?

COMFORT Like it! I'm gonna buy it!

LUC Buy it?

DAVID (*Grinning*) Do you think you can swing it?

COMFORT If I can't, my old man can. He'd like to buy me a place like this to settle down in. I'm a headache for him in Tulsa.

LUC Your father?

COMFORT Sure. Why do you think he sent me to Europe?

MIKE Thank God he did. Look, Comfort, if you're going to buy a place like this, why not be a little more practical? It gets awfully hot in August.

COMFORT What do you want me to buy?

MIKE How about Switzerland? It's a little bigger, but we both like to ski.

COMFORT It's an idea. David, do you think I ought to buy Switzerland for Mike?

DAVID I think he'd be terribly touched.

COMFORT Mike, honey, I'll buy you Switzerland, if that's what you want.

MIKE Ah, you're so good to me. And I'm *so* deserving.

DAVID So very deserving!

(DAVID *and* MIKE *begin to sing* "Be My Host" *in harmony*)

DAVID *and* MIKE (*Sing*)

Anyone with money can go throwing it around,
All around, all around, on the ground.
Anyone with money should be smart enough to see
There are people who need it, like me.

MIKE (*Sings*)

I've discovered how I want to live.

DAVID (*Sings*)

It's more blessed to receive than give.

DAVID *and* MIKE (*Sing*)

Step up, my friend, and be my host.
Step up, and offer me a toast.
I'm the duckiest little guest you ever met.
You're the luckiest—as of yet.
Step up, and proffer me your all.
Step up, and have myself a ball.
As recipient of the best I am the most.
Be my host, be my host, be my host.
Be my host!

(COMFORT *picks up from the boys and sings a second chorus of* "Be My Host," *in which she is joined by several Musicians who come wandering on. At the end of the chorus, as the music continues,* COMFORT *pulls sheafs of money out of her bag and begins to do her own gay, polite version of a fan dance, as* MIKE *and* DAVID *assume the roles of barkers and call out to the race-watchers and passersby*)

MIKE Step up, step up, my friends, and meet our gracious hostess, that charming little philanthropist from Tulsa, Oklahoma, who spends money as though it were going out of style!

DAVID She's an open-handed, free-handed—

MIKE Open-hearted, large-hearted—

DAVID Big-hearted—

MIKE Great-hearted—

DAVID Prodigal lady bountiful!

MIKE And what she's got, she spreads around!

DAVID With joy!

MIKE For kicks!

DAVID Step up, step up with outstretched palms! She's the original cheerful giver—

MIKE She is lavish—

DAVID She's ungrudging—

MIKE She's unsparing—

DAVID She's unstinting—

MIKE *and* DAVID (*Together*) She's your host!
(*By now the stage is filled with moving, dancing people, following* COMFORT, *chasing her, taking money from her,*

passing it around, with her enthusiastic cooperation. Finally, she manages to get rid of them all, and the music comes to an end. JEANETTE *enters, laden and bedecked with all sorts of photographers' paraphernalia, carrying a leather equipment case. At the other side of the stage,* LUC *and* GABRIELLE *are lovingly intertwined, but* JEANETTE *doesn't see them. She calls out gaily*)

JEANETTE Allô! Allô, David!

DAVID (*Going to her*) Well, Jeanette! (*And then, suddenly aware, he shouts*) Jeanette!

MIKE (*Yells to* LUC) Hey, Jeanette!

(LUC *frees himself quickly and speeds to another part of the stage.* DAVID, *to cover, leads* JEANETTE *to* COMFORT)

DAVID Jeanette, this is Comfort O'Connell, aussi une Americaine. Elle vient de Tulsa, Oklahoma.

COMFORT Hello, honey.

JEANETTE Bonjour.

COMFORT What's all that stuff?

MIKE Jeanette is . . . uh . . . uh . . . Luc's . . . assistant.

(COMFORT *looks over at* LUC *with a broad grin and advances on him*)

COMFORT Why, you dirty dog. Two dames. So it's true what they say about you skinny little guys.

(LUC *ducks away and goes to get hold of* JEANETTE. *At the same time,* DAVID *takes* GABRIELLE *by the arm*)

DAVID Come on! Let's go catch the end of the race.

(*But* GABRIELLE *breaks away*)

LUC (*To* JEANETTE, *angrily*) Qu'est-ce que tu fais ici?

JEANETTE Mais, tu as des photos à faire.

LUC Pas tout de suite!

JEANETTE Non, je suis en avance.

MIKE (*Knowing when to get out*) Come on, Comfort, let's go see where the action is.

(*He starts to pull her off stage, but she resists*)

COMFORT I know where the action is, it's right there. I'm no fool!

(DAVID *gives* MIKE *a hand, and together they pull* COMFORT *away*)

DAVID Off we go, Comfort.

COMFORT But I want to see what he does with the two dames!

(*And they are gone.* LUC *glances at* GABRIELLE, *then at* JEANETTE, *who stands cheerfully innocent*)

LUC Je te verrai plus tard.

JEANETTE O.K. Bye-bye.

LUC Pourquoi arrives-tu sitôt?

JEANETTE Mais je croyais tout arranger pour toi.

GABRIELLE Chéri? Tu viens?

LUC (*To* JEANETTE, *uneasily*) Tu comprends . . . il faut que je . . .

JEANETTE Mais oui, ça va, va-t-en. Ne t'inquiètes pas.

LUC (*Angrily*) Je ne m'inquiète pas! Tu veux que je la mette dans un taxi? Oui?

JEANETTE Mais non, Luc! Ne te gâches pas les choses. Elle est charmante. Un beau châssis. Un peu grande pour toi, peut-être. Mais sauves-toi! Amuses-toi! Tout sera prêt à ton retour, je te le promets.

LUC Nom d'un chien! (*He turns and takes* GABRIELLE *off.* JEANETTE *laughs. Off, we can hear* LUC *saying something to* GABRIELLE *that sounds like:* "Allez, Gabrielle. Je téléphonerai plus tard." *And then* LUC *comes stalking back on stage and walks past* JEANETTE) Viens! Prépares l'appareil. Je n'ai pas le temps.

JEANETTE (*With a lovely bow*) Pour toi, n'importe quoi.

LUC She says "Anything for me." Alors, qu'est-ce que tu attends?

JEANETTE (*With a magnificent sweep*) A vos ordres, Maître! Je suis votre esclave.

LUC She says she is my slave, and I her master.

(*The music has begun, and now* JEANETTE *sings the verse of* "La La La")

JEANETTE (*Sings*)

Cett' jolie poupée, c'est moi.

LUC She says she's a doll.

JEANETTE (*Sings*)

Jolie à croquer, c'est moi.

LUC She says she's—
(*He kisses his fingers*)

JEANETTE (*Sings*)

Je n'suis qu'une jolie poupée,
Mais c'est assez, bien assez.

LUC She says— (*He looks at her reproachfully*) ah, no!

JEANETTE (*Gaily*) Ah, oui! (*And she goes into the Refrain, singing*)

La-la-la-la-la,
Je suis mignonne,
Et tout me sourit.

LUC She says: "La-la-la-la-la—"

JEANETTE (*Interrupting, singing*)

La-la-la-la-la,
Il n'y a personne
Qui soit si joli.

LUC She says there's no one in the world who—

JEANETTE (*Interrupting, singing*)

Même la grande Duse,
Elle m'aurait envié,
Car je suis la Muse
De la Beauté.

LUC She says she's—
(*But that's as far as he can get*)

JEANETTE (*Interrupting, singing*)
La-la-la-la-la,
Je suis jolie, mais je n'y suis pour rien:

LUC Here's why!

JEANETTE (*Singing*)
Tout' ma joie me vient de toi. Ah!
C'est toi qui m'vas bien.
La-la-la
C'est toi qui m'vas bien.
(*And now* LUC *happily sings his own chorus*)

LUC (*Sings*)
La-la-la-la-la,
She's nice to look at,
Angels made her dance.

JEANETTE Il dit: "La-la-la-la-la—"

LUC (*Interrupts, singing*)
La-la-la-la-la,
But there's no book at
Which she's had a glance.

JEANETTE Il dit que je n'ai jamais lu un livre.

LUC (*Interrupts, singing*)
Angels never read much;
They just live on love.

JEANETTE Qu'est-ce que c'est "love"?

LUC (*Sings*)

So I never need much
If I plead much.

JEANETTE (*Trying hard to get it all in*) Il dit que j'aime aimer, et que je lui donne tout ce qu'il veut!

LUC (*Interrupting, singing*)

La-la-la-la-la,
Perhaps I boast but
Warm as toast is she.

JEANETTE C'est moi.

LUC

Not quite bright,
But that's all right,
She's ahead of me,
La-la-la,
Far ahead of me!

JEANETTE (*Singing along on the last line*)

Bien au-dessus de lui!

(*And now, having declared their bilingual love, they dance together happily, and disappear. The stage goes dark, Monte Carlo is gone, and suddenly we are back in the photographic studio in Paris, and a wave of people sweep in. We are at* LUC'S *party for* COMFORT. MIKE *and* DAVID *come speeding through the crowd, with* COMFORT *between them, introducing her as they go*)

COMFORT Hey, what a party! I've never met so many people in my life!

MIKE That's what you wanted.

COMFORT I know, but how do I remember their names?

DAVID You don't have to; they won't remember yours.

MIKE There are the Monels: Jack and Maria.

COMFORT Which is which?

MIKE Have you met Comfort O'Connell?

COMFORT I'm awfully glad to meet you! I've heard so much about you!

DAVID If you have, don't repeat it.

COMFORT Where's Luc?

MIKE Somewhere in this mob.

COMFORT Who's that? The tall, thin dame in black with the pearls?

DAVID The Comtesse de Blevard.

COMFORT Is she famous?

DAVID She has three lovers.

COMFORT Well, at least busy.

MIKE Comtesse! This is Comfort O'Connell!

COMFORT Good luck! To all four of you!

(*Let it be noted that up to now, no one spoken to or spoken of has taken any notice of them.* MIKE *quickly turns* COMFORT *away.* DAVID *goes to get another drink*)

DAVID Hey, waiter!

(MOLLIE *appears, pushing her way through the crowd.* LUC *appears, and sees her*)

MOLLIE Excuse me.

LUC Mollie, you're here! Where is Baba?

MOLLIE She's coming. Luc, where did you get the money to throw a party like this?

LUC I have a side line: filthy pictures. You remember David Jordan.

MOLLIE Vividly.

LUC And Mike Robinson. And this is Comfort O'Connell.

MOLLIE Oh, you're the little girl—

COMFORT With the great big bankroll. Yes, ma'am. Word sure gets around, doesn't it?

MOLLIE It sure does.

LUC Come, let's have a drink.

MIKE Miss Plummer is an editor of *Vogue.*

COMFORT Oh, but *Vogue* is my bible!

MOLLIE I know, nobody reads it to see what to wear; it's religious.

(*They go into the crowd.* BARBARA *appears, and* DAVID *sees her, comes alive and crosses to her quickly*)

DAVID Hello.

BARBARA Hello.

DAVID I'm happy to see you again. You look wonderful.

BARBARA Thank you.

DAVID Luc wasn't sure you were coming.

BARBARA Oh, I insisted on coming.

DAVID I've thought of you often, since that day; the day I walked you home.

BARBARA I've thought of it too. It was a lovely walk.

DAVID The best walk two people ever took through Paris. Look, will you have dinner with me tonight? Luc won't mind if we don't stay here long.

BARBARA Oh, but I came with someone.

DAVID Only Mollie. She won't care.
(LOUIS DE POURTAL *enters, looks about, and then sees* BARBARA)

LOUIS Ah, there you are, Baba.
(*He crosses to them*)

BARBARA (*Slightly embarrassed*) Oh, Louis, you know David Jordan. I've heard you speak of him.

LOUIS Yes, of course. Good evening, David. (*To* BARBARA) I called Maxim's and said we would be there about nine-thirty.

BARBARA All right, dear.

(LUC *sees* LOUIS *and crosses to them swiftly*)

LUC Ah, Monsieur de Pourtal, how marvelous of you to come.

LOUIS I was gently persuaded.

LUC (*To* BARBARA) I like that.

(*He takes her hand and moves her across to admire her better and helps her off with the evening coat.* MOLLIE *goes over to inspect the dress*)

MOLLIE Let me see, dear.

LUC Marvelous!

MOLLIE Do you know Comfort O'Connell? And Mike Robinson. This is Barbara Woodruff.

COMFORT (*To* BARBARA) But I know you! I've seen you on *Vogue!* (*She does a quick model's pose*) Oh, you're great!

(*At the same time,* LUC *goes back to* LOUIS)

LUC Monsieur de Pourtal, let me show you what I have as champagne.

(DAVID *moves away. At the same time* LOUIS *hesitates and turns back for a moment*)

LOUIS Baba?

BARBARA I'll find you, Louis.

(LUC *moves* LOUIS *out of the scene*)

LUC (*As they go*) I promise you, you have never tasted champagne like this.

COMFORT (*At the same time, to* MOLLIE) But I thought she was French.

MOLLIE No, she speaks French. I gather that you are the money behind this gala of Luc's.

COMFORT Only the liquor.

MOLLIE What else is there? Well, if you want to break into the Paris underworld, this is the way. Have you met everybody?

COMFORT If I haven't, they're under the tables.

MOLLIE Oh, well, then you've still some perfectly charming people to meet. Come along!

(*She gives* BARBARA *a look and leads* COMFORT *and* MIKE *off into the crowd, leaving* BARBARA *and* DAVID *alone.* BARBARA *remains still, obviously waiting*)

DAVID I once flew a plane for Louis de Pourtal. He had a marvelous girl then, named Anya.

BARBARA Louis has had lots of marvelous girls in his time.

DAVID You bet. And so you have the world. I thought it was something you wanted; I didn't know it was something you had.

BARBARA Yes, I have.

DAVID Good for you.

BARBARA You're not sitting in moral judgment.

DAVID Ah, no! Not that, never that.

BARBARA I've done all right on my own.

DAVID You sure have.

BARBARA I'm the highest-paid model in Paris.

DAVID I know.

BARBARA I buy my own clothes. I pay my own rent.

DAVID I'm sure.

BARBARA Well?

DAVID (*With a wicked grin*) Ah, but all those lovely extras.

BARBARA That's right.
(*A moment*)

DAVID How did you get to Paris?

BARBARA (*Smiles*) I won a dressmaking contest. Does that surprise you? I'm very handy with a needle and thread.

DAVID Nothing about you would surprise me. A dressmaking contest.

BARBARA (*Nods*) One of those big women's magazines back home. And first prize was a round trip to Paris.

DAVID What did you do with the return ticket?

BARBARA Tore it up.

DAVID The very first day.

BARBARA The very first hour. As soon as I'd breathed the air of Paris, I knew I was home. I'd always known it, I think.

DAVID (*Gently, with affection*) How? How would a little girl who'd always lived way uptown in New York know that Paris would have to be home someday?

BARBARA From the things my father told me. Does that surprise you too? My father's a bus driver; he drives a Madison Avenue bus. And in all the years I was growing up, he would come home and tell me of the beautiful ladies with beautiful clothes he had seen up and down Madison Avenue. And then, on my sixteenth birthday—oh, such a beautiful day!—he came home with my present: a two-year subscription to a fashion magazine. And I died. I was lost. And I knew then what my life was going to have to be. (*She smiles at him*) And here I am. Home. (*Pause. He is staring at her*) What is it?

DAVID I've fallen in love with you.

BARBARA (*Trying to keep it light*) Because my father drives a Madison Avenue bus?

DAVID You don't want to hear that, do you?

BARBARA No.

DAVID I can't get you out of my mind.

BARBARA I wish you would try.

DAVID Why? Do I complicate your life?

BARBARA It's just that it wouldn't do any good. (*He turns away. A moment, then she speaks to him gently, rather timidly*) Will you tell me something? Please?

DAVID What?

BARBARA Why you don't write any more? You said you start novels. What stops you?

DAVID The fun of living.

BARBARA Does that make up for not writing?

DAVID Yes. I have a very good time.

BARBARA But you could write too.

DAVID No, I don't seem to have time for both.

BARBARA But you write so beautifully!

DAVID How do you know?

BARBARA That wonderful book you wrote—

DAVID You didn't read it.

BARBARA Yes, I did!
(*And she is caught*)

DAVID Why?

BARBARA I . . . just did.

DAVID After you met me, you went out and bought my book. Why? Why do you care?

BARBARA Naturally, I care. If someone can do something . . .

DAVID Someone? Or me?

BARBARA (*Moving away*) Anyone.

DAVID One book doesn't make a writer, you know.

BARBARA (*Turning back on him*) But I read your short stories too! And they're all good! Every one!

DAVID (*Staring at her*) You found my book of short stories. That's been out of print—

BARBARA I found it.

DAVID (*Advancing on her*) And so you want me to write again.

BARBARA Yes.

DAVID Because you feel I've more to say.

BARBARA Oh, yes!

DAVID And more books to write.

BARBARA I'm sure of it.

DAVID Why do you care? Why? (*He takes her; she attempts to break free, and he holds her*) What are you doing with that lecherous old man? What is it he gives you you can't live without? You're so proud of the fact that you made your own way, why did you blow it? You can't hang a sign around your neck saying, "I pay my own rent." What do you need him for? Stop playing safe!

BARBARA (*Breaking free*) I want to play safe!

DAVID Without love? You said you wanted loads of love. There's no love.

BARBARA You don't know!

DAVID I know! You don't love him.

BARBARA It can wait.

DAVID What? Love? Stop backing away.

BARBARA (*Tensely*) Stop it! Stop telling me what to do! (*The music hits hard, and she is immediately into the song* "You Don't Tell Me")

You don't teach a kid to drink milk,
Or a mack'rel to swim in the sea,
And when the magic hour approaches, lover,
You don't tell me.
You don't teach the ocean to roll,
Or an Englishman how to drink tea,
And when affection starts to take me over,
You don't tell me.

Only yesterday
I was green as May.
Now I have to say
I'm wise to certain symptoms.
The young have an option on youth.
I'm as young as I ever will be.
I really understand the moment of truth.
You don't tell me!

(At the end of the song, LOUIS *appears. The three stand still, separated in space.* BARBARA *looks from* DAVID *to* LOUIS, *then moves across the stage to* LOUIS, *who holds her wrap and puts it on her, and they go off.* MOLLIE *has appeared, strolling on with* MIKE *and* COMFORT, *and they witness the exit of* BARBARA *and* LOUIS)

MOLLIE Barbara, are you going? (*They are gone. She looks at* DAVID *and guesses*) Well, young man—poaching? (*She moves to him and offers him a drink*) You look at though you could use this. (*He takes it and drinks*) You're on the wrong game preserve.

DAVID I don't think so.

MOLLIE Very high walls.

DAVID I'll get over them.

MOLLIE I doubt that very much.

DAVID (*Sardonically*) Love conquers all.

MOLLIE How true. And all the world loves a lover. And all's fair in love and war. And— (*She's stuck. She looks across to* COMFORT) Have you got one, dear?

(COMFORT *is up to the occasion*)

COMFORT (*Bravely*) It is better to have loved and lost, than never to have loved at all.

MOLLIE Well said! (DAVID *hurls his glass at one of* LUC'S *overhead lights and moves swiftly out through the crowd.* MOLLIE *looks after him, then looks at* COMFORT *quizzically.* MIKE *hurries out after* DAVID) Love!

COMFORT Love!

(*A Musician with a trombone wanders on, playing, and* MOLLIE *and* COMFORT *sing* "Love Makes the World Go")

MOLLIE (*Sings*)

Wonderful world of commonplace.
Where each of us knows where he stands.

COMFORT (*Sings*)

Where words have a childish kind of grace
And intellect makes no demands.

MOLLIE *and* COMFORT (*Sing*)

Place where a thought never pays;
Wonderful world of clichés.

(*Refrain*)
The moon is bright when you're in love.
The skies are always fair.
A million stars are spread above.

MOLLIE

Love makes the world go square.
Dumb little words are brilliant

COMFORT

Numb reactions become resilient.

NO STRINGS

MOLLIE *and* COMFORT

Love has such a pretty sound
You have to learn to care.

MOLLIE

If money makes the mare go,

COMFORT

Love makes the world go square.

MOLLIE *and* COMFORT

Love makes the world go square.

MOLLIE

The race is to the swift, my friend,

COMFORT

But haste makes waste, mon cher.

MOLLIE *and* COMFORT

Besides, love laughs at locksmiths.
Love makes the world go square.

MOLLIE

Who needs to think in Maytime?

COMFORT

Zen Buddhism is not for haytime.
Thought is naught and mind is blind

MOLLIE

When music's in the air.
Just murmer low "I love you."

MOLLIE *and* COMFORT

Love makes the world go square.
Love makes the world go square.

(*Towards the end of the second chorus,* MOLLIE *and* COMFORT *move over to the trombonist, and suddenly* MOLLIE *pulls the slide out of the trombone and moves away quickly.* COMFORT *joins her and they escape through the crowd of party guests, who are dancing. The trombonist stares at his raped trombone for a long moment, then starts after them, his finger raised as though calling to them. The music continues, the guests go on dancing.* MOLLIE *appears, still carrying the slide, and scampers across through the crowd and off; and a moment later* COMFORT *follows her, carrying the rest of the trombone. Another moment, and the trombonist comes across following them, his finger still raised, and disappears off after them. The dancing goes on. Now we hear the trombone again, and* MOLLIE *and the trombonist and* COMFORT *appear, moving on, shoulder to shoulder. The trombone is intact again, and he is playing beautifully;* MOLLIE *and* COMFORT *sing another chorus of* "Love Makes The World Go." *They put their fists into the bell of the trombone to quiet it; he steps away, leaving them holding the trombone, and the song ends. The three go off, the dancers begin to scatter, and as they do, the scene changes, they are gone and the party is finished. We are in* BARBARA's *sitting room, later that night. A drum sounds gently, then fades out, and* BARBARA *enters from the bedroom, in negligee. She is somberly thoughtful. She sits and stares into space, then hears a sound and looks off.* DAVID *appears out of darkness and stands looking down at her*)

Diahann Carroll and Richard Kiley as BARBARA WOODRUFF and DAVID JORDAN

DAVID Louis' chauffeur is outside, sitting in the car, watching. I borrowed a match from him.

BARBARA Did you think that was clever?

DAVID No, it just happened that way. If I leave right away and borrow another match, there'll be no harm done.

BARBARA What do you want?

DAVID On the other hand, if I stay for a while, your world may be destroyed.

BARBARA It doesn't destroy that easily.

DAVID Oh, I don't know. Anya used to tell me that Louis cracked quite a whip.

BARBARA What do you want?

DAVID A friend of mine has a small house at Honfleur. Do you know where that is? The Normandy coast. The most beautiful place in France, I think. I can have it for as long as I want.

BARBARA And that would be fun! Great fun!

DAVID Will you come?

BARBARA And destroy my world? No.

DAVID We're involved, now. We can't stop.

BARBARA Yes, I can.

DAVID We're on rails.

BARBARA Please go away.

DAVID Barbara—

BARBARA Please, please, please go away!

DAVID I've nowhere to go; I'm home.

BARBARA (*Desperately*) Go away! I want no part of your life! It's a terrible life!

DAVID I think it's pretty good.

BARBARA You've talked yourself into it! The fair-haired boy of Europe! The nonwriting writer! Everyone's friend! There's always someone who'll give you a house, isn't there? And always a girl to take to it. Not me. Not me.

DAVID What are you slanging me for?

BARBARA You don't need me to help you destroy yourself. You're doing a good job on your own.

DAVID No one's destroyed.

BARBARA (*Miserable, lost*) Yes, you. And me, too, if we're ever together. . . .

DAVID We're already there. Barbara—

BARBARA No! Go away!

DAVID (*Demanding*) What do you want? On your own terms! Say it! What do you want me to do?

BARBARA (*Fiercely*) Live some kind of a life! I hate waste! I hate waste!

DAVID (*Driving*) Say it! What!

BARBARA Stop coasting, stop running, stop hiding!

DAVID With you! Whatever you want, with you! (*He takes hold of her. A moment, and she is in his arms*) From the very first day. From the day I walked you home.

BARBARA But I didn't want it to happen!

DAVID There was no way to stop it.

BARBARA I didn't want to fall in love. (*Lost, almost to herself*) What'll I do? What'll I do?

DAVID (*Gently, quietly*) Nobody ever really wants to fall in love. It isn't something you set out to do. But nobody wants to be alone. (*The music of* "Nobody Told Me" *begins and he sings*)

Night is a lonely time
With no one to sing to.
Night is the only time
When you badly need someone to cling to.
Cling to me, my dear.
Sing to me—all I need made clear.

(*Refrain*)
Nobody told me
Love was made of lightning.
Nobody warned me
Love would make me quake.
No one suggested
I would not be rested

If night after night
I lay awake—alone.
Should they have told me
Love was made of hunger,
Crimson surrounded by blue?
Nobody told me,
No, not even you.
Nobody told me—I knew.

BARBARA (*Sings*)

Nobody told me
Love was like a whirlwind.
Nobody told me
Love would make me weep.
How could they let me
Let this thing upset me
Until I could never fall asleep—till dawn.
Should they have told me
Love would come to own me
Healing and wounding me, too.
Nobody told me,
No, not even you.
Nobody told me—I knew.

(*The sound of drums begins to intrude. The lovers disappear. The drums become more insistent, and take command, and reach a climax. The lovers, in darkness, are enveloped and blanketed in sound*)

Curtain

ACT TWO

ACT TWO

Honfleur: at the edge of the sea on the Normandy coast. It is a bright, sunny day.

DAVID, *in old trousers and an old shirt, is half-sitting, half-lying, staring out to sea.*

BARBARA (*Off*) David? . . . David! . . . Where are you? (DAVID *pays no attention.* BARBARA *comes racing on*) David? (*And then she sees him and goes to him*) Oh, really, David! You could have answered.

DAVID I was guiding you. Silently. Like talking down a plane flying blind, in a fog.

BARBARA I might have crashed and skinned my knee.

DAVID No, I had you tight and safe. In here. (*He taps his head*)

BARBARA I know.

DAVID My head is full of you.

BARBARA But that's wrong! It's supposed to be full of beautiful words and declarative sentences. You're writing. Drive me out.

DAVID I can't.

BARBARA Ah, no, David, don't say that. I'm not a distraction; I'm supposed to be good for you. I don't make a sound when you're writing. And I hide, so you won't see me. Tell me I'm good for you.

DAVID (*Pulling her down to him*) You are the very best for me.

(*He has her in his arms*)

BARBARA And I do help you. The way I make coffee? A writer has to have coffee.

DAVID Oh, such a big help, such marvelous coffee! Ow!

BARBARA What's the matter?

DAVID You're getting awfully bony.

BARBARA Oh, no, those are rocks.

DAVID What?

BARBARA Stones. Look, David, I found them on the beach. Aren't they beautiful? (*She takes them out of her pocket with childish enthusiasm*) Look at them, look at this one. That streak of pink in the gray? It's so beautiful! And this one. So smooth and lovely. Just to touch, just to feel! Take it in your hand.

DAVID Mmmm . . . nice.

BARBARA I held it all the way down the beach. (*A surge of happiness*) Oh, David!

DAVID Keep it. Don't lose it.

BARBARA Oh, I won't!

DAVID And carry it with you, wherever you go. So that when life is drab, you'll have something to touch . . . and to hold. . . .

BARBARA What a lovely idea. A touchstone. But I don't need it. You are my touchstone. I measure the world by you, now. Is it a good day or bad? It depends on how David feels. Hear the sound of the sea, the waves on the shore. Like music? Not if it bothers my David when he's trying to write.

DAVID Darling, turn off the moon, it shines in my eyes.

BARBARA Oh, I will!

(*They hold each other happily and stare out to sea. The music begins, and they drift into the song* "Look No Further")

DAVID (*Sings*)

Look at the ocean,
Look at the sand,
Look at each other with love.
With love we look at each other.
Now we have found what we planned.

(*Refrain*)
Look no further,
Be still.
Don't move an inch away. Stay;
Stay with one who loves you.
Look no further, dear.

BARBARA (*Sings*)

No more searching,
That's through.
This is the journey's end, friend.

Friend has turned to lover.
Look no further, dear.
Why must you wander?
Heaven isn't far.
Rest where you are.
I'm the nearest star.

DAVID

I can see you—right there,
Making me all complete, sweet.
Sweet it is to hold you.
Look no further, dear.

DAVID *and* BARBARA

Look no further, dear.
Why must you wander?
Heaven isn't far.

DAVID

Rest where you are.

BARBARA

I'm the nearest star.

DAVID

I can see you—right there.

BARBARA

Making me all complete.

DAVID

Sweet.

DAVID *and* BARBARA

Sweet it is to hold you.
Look no further, dear.
Look no further, dear.

(The song comes to an end, the music fades out, and they lie close together, staring out to sea)

BARBARA Shall we go home?

DAVID Mmmm. Soon
(BARBARA *frees herself and sits up*)

BARBARA David, you've got to work.

DAVID Mmmm.

BARBARA Look at the beautiful sailboat.

DAVID Mmm.

BARBARA What is it?

DAVID A ketch.

BARBARA A ketch. How can you tell?

DAVID The mizzen's before the wheel.

BARBARA How nice. Oh, the mizzen's before the wheel, tra-la, the mizzen's before the wheel. What's the mizzen?

DAVID The smaller sail aft.

BARBARA And what's that silly little boat with the silly little sail?

DAVID A fishing boat.

BARBARA But that silly little pocket handkerchief of a sail can't do any good.

DAVID No, the boat's got an engine. The spanker's just to hold it steady in the wind.

BARBARA Is that what that sail's called? A spanker?

DAVID Yep.

BARBARA Oh, you know so much.

DAVID Yep. A fund of knowledge.

BARBARA It's because you're a stern and rock-bound coast-of-Maine man, that's why, isn't it?

DAVID Yep.

BARBARA Tell me more.

DAVID What?

BARBARA About how stern and rock-bound you are.

DAVID I'm only stern; you're the one that's rock-bound.

BARBARA Do the lobster boats on the coast of Maine wear spankers?

DAVID Some do, some don't.

BARBARA That's a good answer. If I were a lobsterman, I'd have all my boats wear spankers.

DAVID Run up by Dior, of course.

BARBARA Of course. And Balmain and Balenciaga and Givenchy. I'd have them all make me spankers in the most beautiful colors. Would they like that in Maine?

DAVID They would adore it.

BARBARA What would they say? When they saw my beautiful spankers?

DAVID Well . . . they might say . . . (*In a good Maine accent*) "Crotch-a-mighty! That girl's right up on her bean-water, ain't she?"

BARBARA (*With amazed delight*) Right up on her what?

DAVID Bean-water.

BARBARA Crotch-a-mighty! What does it mean?

DAVID Oh . . . sort of frisky.

BARBARA Oh, I like it. I'm right up on my bean-water, today.

DAVID You sure are. And you're slick as a schoolmarm's leg too.

BARBARA David, not really! Slick as a schoolmarm's leg? They don't really say that.

DAVID Not any more. But I heard an old fisherman say it once, and it stuck.

BARBARA You remember it all, don't you? Everything out of your childhood.

DAVID No, not all; I wish I did. But little things like that come back.

BARBARA And what was the name of that tree that grows there? The wonderful name that I loved so?

DAVID Hackmatack.

BARBARA A hackmatack tree! I picture Maine as being covered with hackmatack trees!

DAVID (*With a touch of Maine*) Nope. Pine and spruce, birch and cedar, mostly. Why do you love it so? When I talk of Maine?

BARBARA Because it's you. The things that say "home" to you. I'm jealous, I guess.

DAVID No home for you to remember but Paris?

BARBARA No, that's not true . . . completely. I have nice memories of home. Some. But no hackmatack trees.

DAVID They probably grow in Central Park.

BARBARA We did have geraniums on the fire escape, though.

DAVID Now, that makes *me* jealous.

BARBARA Didn't you have geraniums?

DAVID We didn't have fire escapes.

BARBARA Oh, how sad! How about sidewalks?

DAVID Nope.

BARBARA Oh, no sidewalks! You poor, underprivileged thing! Only sea and sky and trees and rocks and boats on the water! How could you bear it?

DAVID I don't rightly know. But I did.
(*Sings* "Maine")
Let the snow come down
Before the sun comes up.
Maine is the main thing.
Let the lake and hills
Become a frozen cup.
Twenty below in Maine.
Get the sleigh, turn about.
That's a nice team.
Make believe all of it's yours.
Take a breath, blow it out,
No, it ain't steam.
It'll be warmer indoors.
Let the snow come down
Before it starts to rain.
Under the covers—it's cozy.
Far away, cross the bay
Goes an old train:
Woo-hoo, woo-hoo.
(*Sound of train*)
Mainly I do like Maine.

BARBARA (*Sings*)
When the sun goes down
The kids are up and out,

East of the Hudson.
There's a sidewalk symphony
Of song and shout
Up north of Central Park.
When it's late, climb the stairs,
Ready for bed.
Close your eyes, start to count sheep.
Music comes floating up into your head,
What's the use trying to sleep?
There's a record playing in the flat below,
Down there a trumpet blows softly.
What a warm place it is after it's dark.
Wah-hoo, wah-hoo.
(*Sound of trumpet*)
Up north of Central Park.

DAVID	BARBARA
Let the snow come down Before the sun comes up.	When the sun goes down The kids are out!
Maine is the main thing! Let the lake and hills get frozen up,	Where's Maine? There's a sidewalk symphony Of song and shout
Way up in Maine.	Up north of Central Park.
Get the sleigh, turn about. That's a nice team.	Close your eyes, start to count sheep.

DAVID *and* BARBARA

Warm or cold what's the use turnin' on steam?
Never mind trying to sleep.

DAVID
Let the snow come down
Before it starts to rain
Under the covers

BARBARA
There's a record playing in
the flat below.

DAVID *and* BARBARA
It's cozy!
What a warm place it is
after it's dark!

DAVID
Woo-hoo! Woo-hoo!
Mainly I do like—
Mainly I do like—
Mainly I do like—
Maine. . . .

BARBARA
Wah-hoo! Wah-hoo!
Up north of Central—
Up north of Central—
Up north of Central—
Central Park!

DAVID Let's do something exciting this afternoon.

BARBARA All right, I know just the thing.

DAVID What?

BARBARA We'll go home, and you'll write.

DAVID Ah, no, I don't feel like it. Let's go sailing.

BARBARA David, you've got to work.

DAVID But it's the weekend!

BARBARA What difference does that make?

DAVID And Easter weekend, at that! No one works Easter weekend.

BARBARA You do.

DAVID Look, what about Deauville?

BARBARA What about it?

DAVID It's right there 'round the corner, less than ten miles down the coast. And this is the weekend for Deauville. Everyone's there.

BARBARA I like it here.

DAVID Now, Baba, you know what it's like Easter weekend. The best house party of the year. Gay! Gala! Let's have some fun. Just for the night. We'll go for dinner, see the gala and dance, do some gambling, say hello to everyone we know, and come home. What's wrong with that?

BARBARA No.

DAVID No?

BARBARA No. (*Lightly*) Besides, I'd already said no.

DAVID To what?

BARBARA Deauville.

(*The scene changes, during the following, and they approach their room, which opens off a terrace and looks out over the sea*)

DAVID When?

BARBARA Mollie asked me. She's taking some models to Deauville this weekend, with Luc, to shoot fashions around the Casino.

DAVID When did she ask you?

BARBARA Oh, almost two weeks ago.

DAVID (*Annoyed*) Why didn't you tell me?

BARBARA I didn't see any point.

DAVID What did you say?

BARBARA I said I was awfully sorry, I'm not modeling these days, because we're writing a novel.

(*And the open, innocent confidence of the way she says it makes* DAVID *laugh. He stops and faces her and takes her by the arms and looks at her searchingly*)

DAVID We have another saying in Maine. It isn't said often.

BARBARA What?

DAVID "I don't have to look no higher'n your head for my savior."

(*She smiles her pleasure, and he kisses her on the brow. The scenery has finished changing, and they are home. They separate. Barbara touches him gently, then heads into the house*)

BARBARA I'll go make you some coffee. (*She runs into the house. The light begins to fade. Wisps of fog roll in.* DAVID *stands alone, staring out to sea. As the light dims, we hear the faint stirrings of* "Be My Host," *as though echoing in his mind. And then we hear an echo of* "Look No Further," *and the two melodies clash, and figures move through the gathering dusk, and are gone. It is dusk, now.* DAVID *sits down at his typewriter, inserts a piece of paper, turns the roller, and keeps turning it, in reverie, until the paper falls out. The music from Deauville intrudes again, and then over it, in the distance, we hear* BARBARA *singing a small part of* "Look No Further." DAVID *puts the paper back in the typewriter and starts to type. Figures begin to drift on from the darkness:* DAVID'S *pals in Deauville, brightly dressed, their faces blank.* DAVID *gets stuck, begins to hit one key. The Deauville music becomes more insistent, and he keeps pounding at the one key with growing anger, and finally, desperately, he pulls the paper from the typewriter and crumples it.* BARBARA *appears with coffee. The music cuts off*) Darling, you've no light!

DAVID It's all right.

BARBARA But you can't see to write! (*She makes a move, and there is light*) There. How's it going?

DAVID Fine.

BARBARA Is there anything I can do?

DAVID No.

BARBARA Sharpen some pencils?

DAVID No.

BARBARA Oh, I'm bothering you.

DAVID No.

BARBARA David, what is it?

DAVID Nothing.

BARBARA You're stuck. I know. But you mustn't get angry. Everyone gets stuck once in a while. You told me yourself, it happens to everyone. . . . (*He turns away. She watches him anxiously*) Darling, you're just having a bad day—

HIS PALS (*Echoing*) Having a bad day—having a bad day—

BARBARA Everyone has a bad day. But tomorrow—

DAVID What tomorrow?

BARBARA (*Trying hard to be bright*) David, do you know what I hope you got in? That story you told me about the day the skunk fell into the quarry, and your father got hold of that great big derrick with the bucket—what did you call it? And oh, David . . . I keep thinking of your uncles in their little boats . . . moving out through the islands of Jericho Bay . . .

DAVID I'm not writing about Maine.

BARBARA But you are!

DAVID I said I'm not. I threw it away the first week.

BARBARA (*Frightened*) Why?

DAVID It wasn't any good.

BARBARA That's not true!

DAVID What do you know?

BARBARA But all those wonderful stories you've told me—

DAVID It wasn't any good. When I came to write it, it wasn't any good.

BARBARA But David—

DAVID Will you stop pushing at me! What the hell do you know? I couldn't write it. I couldn't!
(*Pause*)

BARBARA (*Quietly*) But you've been writing.

DAVID Oh, yes.

BARBARA What?

DAVID I've started another novel.

BARBARA About what?

DAVID Oh . . . just . . . people . . . my pals

HIS PALS Hey!

BARBARA Doing what?

DAVID Oh . . . just knocking around Europe. The things I know. (*Ironically. He has been avoiding her eyes*) You're supposed to write about the things you know.

BARBARA What's there to know? (*Desperately*) David! There's nothing to know! What can you write about those people?

DAVID I know all about them!

BARBARA There's nothing to know! Your pals? Your gay pals? They devour you! They go from Paris to Rome to Cannes to Biarritz and back to Paris. And what have they done? Nothing. And what have they seen? Each other. What have you got to write about?

DAVID (*Fiercely*) What do you want me to do?
(*The music of Deauville begins to intrude again*)

BARBARA Write about the things you really know! The things in your bones, and in your blood!

DAVID I told you I tried! It wasn't any good!

BARBARA What kind of a try did you make?

DAVID What the hell do you know about how a man tries?

BARBARA Did you try? And quit in less than a week? Is that what you call a try?

DAVID I've been trying for years, can't you see?

BARBARA (*Close to tears*) No, I can't! You're a coward! A quitter! You don't know how to try! You're licked before you begin!

DAVID That's right. You're right. I'm licked.

BARBARA No, David—

DAVID Oh, yes, you're right about something else, too, the book about Europe. It's no good, it's no goddamned good; nothing I touch is good; I've forgotten how to write! It's been so long since I wrote anything decent, I've forgotten how!

BARBARA David—

DAVID Why do you think I run? I start something and decide it stinks and throw it away and run! So stop wasting your time!

BARBARA If you'll only be patient and try—

DAVID Oh, you've got it all taped, haven't you? Baba knows best! Always so right, so goddamned right!

(He starts away fast. The music is strong and insistent now)

BARBARA Where are you going?

DAVID To be devoured by my pals!

BARBARA *(Frantically)* David, where are you going?

DAVID Where the action is! Where everybody is! There's no action here!

(And his pals sweep around him and carry him off. The idyllic little house by the sea breaks up and disappears, and BARBARA *is gone. Figures appear in a bright light, and the music is loud and strong, and a ballet leads us into Deauville. The end of the dance brings* DAVID *on, scenery drops into place, and we are in the Deauville Casino. Suddenly, out of the action and movement, we find* MIKE *and* COMFORT*)*

COMFORT Hey, David! Where've you been hiding?

(She kisses him enthusiastically)

DAVID Hi, Comfort.
(He shakes hands with MIKE*)*

COMFORT Hey, this Deauville! I like this Casino even better than Monte Carlo!

MIKE Dave, she keeps winning. How do you like that? I can't make a quarter, and every time she turns around, she picks up a couple of thousand francs.

FIRST CROUPIER Vingt-deux, noir.

COMFORT Hey, that's me! Here, boys, go play at another table; you'll cramp my style. *(She hands them stacks of plaques, and races back to her table)* And play a number for me. Sixteen. That was my age when I first got . . . lucky.

MIKE *(To* DAVID*)* What happened to you and Barbara?

DAVID I blew it.

MIKE It was bound to happen.

DAVID I blew it. Me.

MIKE You listen to your Uncle Michael, boy. True love never bought any groceries. Come on.
(They go to a roulette table)

FIRST CROUPIER Dix-sept, noir!

COMFORT Hey, Mike! I won again!

MIKE How do you like that!

DAVID Everything on zero!
(*The wheels turn, the ball bounces and drops into place*)

SECOND CROUPIER Le numéro seize.

MIKE Hey, Comfort! It came up! I was all over sixteen!

COMFORT That's my boy!

DAVID Zero again.
(*The wheels turn, the ball drops*)

SECOND CROUPIER C'est le zéro.

DAVID Hey, I won!

MIKE You see, David, you're alive again!

DAVID Comfort, you brought me luck!

COMFORT That's my mission in life. What number did you play?

DAVID Zero!

COMFORT That's a number?

DAVID Come on, let's get out of here, let's move on.

COMFORT Sure! Where do you want to go?

MIKE How about St. Tropez?

DAVID That's what we want—St. Tropez!

COMFORT Will we know anybody?

MIKE Anybody!

DAVID Everybody!
(They dash out with part of the crowd. The Casino begins to disappear, the crowd thins out, and suddenly everything is gone, and the scene changes to BARBARA'S *apartment.* BARBARA *appears, and then, after a moment)*

MOLLIE *(Off)* Knock, knock, I'm here.

BARBARA Mollie?

MOLLIE *(As she enters)* Hello, my darling. Welcome back to Paris. I've missed you.

BARBARA *(Almost tearfully)* Oh, Mollie, I'm so glad to see you!

MOLLIE Now, Barbara, don't look like that! It gives you wrinkles up here. *(She touches the corners of her eyes)* And then you have to read the article I wrote on what to do about it. And I don't really know. Come, tell me all. *(She leads* BARBARA *to the sofa)* How do you feel?

BARBARA Miserable.

MOLLIE That's nonsense. Haven't you ever had a man walk out on you before? It's no worse than a bad cold. What I always do: I soak in a hot tub until I'm all shriveled up—

BARBARA *(Stopping her)* Mollie . . . I want him back.

MOLLIE The trouble is, he'll *be* back. Why did he walk out?

BARBARA Oh . . . he was having a bad time trying to write . . .

MOLLIE And you kept pushing at him. I know. There's nothing like the inspiration of a good woman to make a man leave home.

BARBARA But Mollie, he *can write*. I gave you his book and his short stories; you're an editor; you should know.

MOLLIE Oh, yes, he can write like a streak, the fool. What a waste.

BARBARA Well, then, if he's with me, if I *take* him someplace—

MOLLIE You tried that once; did it work? You could take him to the bottom of the Mediterranean, and he'd find some fish that was throwing a party.

BARBARA And so the hell with him?

MOLLIE Barbara, if he turns up again, there's only one thing you can do for him, the very best thing: send him home.

BARBARA Home!

MOLLIE Back to America, to work. It's the only thing that can save him. Life's too easy for him here. Send him home.

BARBARA But I love him!

MOLLIE Especially if you love him. If you love him, I'll tell you what you must say to him: three little words, and they're not I love you: "Yankee, go home." (*She goes to her bag*) You stop by the office tomorrow, dear. I want to put you to work, again.

BARBARA All right, Mollie.

(LOUIS *appears, and* MOLLIE *gives him a deep bow*)

MOLLIE Darling, here's the mender of broken dreams.

LOUIS (*Amused*) Mollie . . .

MOLLIE How nice to know there are some things one can depend on—like money. Louis, could I borrow your car to take me to the office?

LOUIS Yes, of course.

MOLLIE Good man.

(*She goes*)

LOUIS How are you, Barbara?

BARBARA I've been ditched, Louis. You've heard about it.

LOUIS That's why I'm here.

BARBARA You don't want me back; I've treated you so shabbily.

LOUIS I believe every girl is entitled to one romantic mistake.

BARBARA And mine was really a beaut, wasn't it?

LOUIS Come back, Barbara. Be wise.

BARBARA I don't know how, that's my trouble. I've never been wise.

LOUIS David Jordan's not for you. He'll never be able to take care of you. Most Americans who come to live in Europe at least make a lot of money and hide it away in Switzerland. But not him. He's even a failure as an expatriate.

BARBARA Louis, if he were to come back tomorrow, I would leave you again. I couldn't do that to you; it would be such a dirty trick. But thank you for asking.

LOUIS (*With a good-humored shrug*) Well. And so I must find a new pupil.

BARBARA (*Smiling*) That shouldn't be hard.

LOUIS No. But you were something special. You even learned the difference between Cezanne and Picasso.

BARBARA (*Brightly*) Oh, that was easy! Cezanne painted apples, Picasso painted women with three of everything.

LOUIS (*Laughs and kisses her hand*) Goodbye, my star pupil.

BARBARA Goodbye, Louis.

LOUIS And remember: the red wine must never be chilled.
(*He turns and goes. She is alone, and the smile fades; she stares across the room. The music begins:* "An Orthodox Fool")

BARBARA (*Sings*)
If I stood over there and looked my way,
What a pitiful sight I'd see.
Stupid, stupider, stupidest—
This is the declension
Of little declining me.

(*Refrain*)
I'm a self-educated idiot,
I'm an orthodox fool.
All I'm not I owe to myself.
Ev'ry discredit should go to myself.
I knew my way but I lost it;
The game was won but I tossed it.
I knew the speech but I mumbled;
I caught the ball but I fumbled.
I'm a young victim of senility;
I am destiny's tool.
I am lucky that the world has me alive in it—
If the swimming pool is empty then I dive in it,
With my tarnished golden rule,
I am dumb, obtuse, absurd and blind.
I'm an orthodox fool!
(*The music shifts to the strain of* "Nobody Told Me" *and she sings*)
Should they have told me
Love would come to own me,
Healing and wounding me too.
Nobody told me,
No, not even you.
Nobody told me—I knew.
(*The music suddenly shifts back to* "An Orthodox Fool" *and she sings*)
I'm a clear picture of incompetence
Who was fired from school.
I put money in the market when it's slowing up,
I descend the escalator when it's going up.
Like a slightly well-read mule
I am dull, benumbed and not quite bright.
I'm an orthodox fool.

A crazy, mixed-up, card-carrying dope,
A thick-headed, dimwitted, brain of soap,
A self-educated idiot,
I'm an orthodox fool! Fool! Fool!

(The song ends, she is gone, and suddenly the stage is flooded with Mediterranean sunlight, and COMFORT *appears. She wears a short bolero that stops just below the breasts, and short, skin-tight, Western-style pants that sit low on the hips. Her midriff is bare. She looks bored. More girls come strolling on; they are almost completely undressed, since we are on a beach near St. Tropez. There's not much scenery: a few beach chairs, a low wooden painted slat fence that is carried on by some of the beach boys who appear.* MIKE *comes on, wearing an old shirt and a pair of cotton pants, carrying the portable bar. He wears, too, a battered sailor's hat. He makes himself comfortable, and then we discover* DAVID, *farther back, lounging back on a beach chair, surrounded by girls.* MIKE *keeps eying the passing girls with interest, and when one of them happens to stop nearby, with her back to him, and bends over to adjust her beach shoe, he takes off his hat and places it over his heart, being a true, patriotic gentleman. During all this, the music has been growing more and more insistent, and now* COMFORT *starts to sing* "Eager Beaver")

COMFORT

I'm sick of Dullsville;
I'd rather be in Deauville,
Where people and roulette wheels go flashing by.
You don't want placid grandeur,
So give me your hand, you're
Just as anxious to keep moving as I!

(*Refrain*)
What makes an eager beaver eager to be busy?
What makes an eager beaver try to jump the gun?
Maybe a beaver thinks a bit of rest
Might cause a mild revulsion,
Or does a feeling of compulsion
Make him run, run, run?
Come, little beaver, I believe a task awaits us.
Each little nibble brings you close to where I am.
Build like a beaver 'till the thing we're building mates us.
Eager beavers always give a dam.
Nice little beaver with the skin so soft,
Nice little beaver with the teeth so white,
Beaver! Beaver, we're right!

Come on, what's the action? Hey, David, what have we got for today?

DAVID I don't know. Mike?

MIKE First we're going to Pamplona to swim, then over to Roches Fleuries for lunch—

DAVID How about some skin-diving off the Lazareff rocks?

MIKE Sure. Then back to Beauvallon to have cocktails with the Chauvels, then we're going to drive to Cannes for dinner. And gamble.

COMFORT That's all?

MIKE That's all?!

COMFORT (*Sings*)
Action. Action.
Lovely, lively action.

MIKE (*Sings*)

A word that often has the prefix "re-";

MIKE *and* COMFORT

Reaction. Reaction,
The best part is reaction.
It's like the breath of life to you and me.

MIKE

"Hurry" is the word as well as "busy."

COMFORT

Hasten, keep your face in line with mine.

MIKE *and* COMFORT

We can stop each other getting dizzy,
But dizziness can often be divine.
Action. Reaction!
Action. Reaction!

MIKE (*Sings*)

What makes an eager beaver eager to be busy?
What makes an eager beaver try to jump the gun?
Maybe a beaver thinks a bit of rest
Might cause a mild revulsion,
Or does a feeling of compulsion
Make him run, run, run?
Come, little beaver, I believe a task awaits us.
Each little nibble brings you close to where I am.
Build like a beaver 'till the thing we're building mates us.
Eager beavers always give a dam.
Nice little beaver with the skin so soft,

Nice little beaver with the teeth so white,
Beaver! Beaver, we're right!

(*The music continues, and the girls and beach boys start to dance, and in the ensuing melee,* COMFORT *and* MIKE *get separated, and* MIKE *disappears with a girl he has been eying. The music ends, and* COMFORT *starts looking around for* MIKE)

COMFORT Mike? Mike? Hey, David, what happened to Mike?

(*The girls and boys begin to wander off, taking the chairs with them*)

DAVID I don't know. He was here a minute ago. (*He is making himself a drink*) He probably went to get some cigarettes.

COMFORT You can get cigarettes right over there. (*She is moving about anxiously*) Mike? . . . Mike? . . . (*By now the crowd is almost gone, and the last to go are a couple of beach boys who carry away the slatted wooden fence.* COMFORT *discovers* MIKE, *on the ground with the girl*) You two-timing, double-crossing son-of-a-bitch.

(MIKE *rises quickly, shooing the girl off and away*)

MIKE Hello, honey, I was just admiring the view.

COMFORT I saw you admiring the view.

MIKE (*Coming to her*) Now, Comfort, don't get excited.

COMFORT Get the hell out of here. Get out of my life.

MIKE It was just one of those little accidents. You know what I mean.

COMFORT It wasn't an accident! I've seen you looking around.

MIKE Who, me? Honey, I swear—

COMFORT No man's going to treat me like a wife!

MIKE Now, Comfort—

COMFORT If what you're getting from me isn't enough—

MIKE Honey, it is! Look! I didn't want it! If I could give it back to her, I'd do it!

(*And with that she slaps him hard. Livid with anger, he goes to slap her back, but* DAVID *grabs his arm*)

DAVID Hey!

MIKE I don't like women slapping me!

COMFORT Not even with hundred-dollar bills in their hands? (*A long, hard pause*) Get out of my life. You know where your clothes are. Get 'em and pack. Just get out of my life.

(MIKE *attempts and manages, with some effort, a gay, nonchalant, insouciant smile*)

MIKE Well, back to Rome and those lousy Italian movies. See you on the Via Veneto, David.

(*And he turns and trots off. A moment, then* COMFORT *turns to* DAVID, *and manages a brave smile*)

COMFORT That leaves you and me, David. Let's get out of here, huh? I don't think much of this place. Where would you like to go? Greece? Turkey? How about Vienna? I haven't been to Vienna, yet. Is there any action there?

DAVID (*Gently*) Comfort, you don't need me.

COMFORT But I like you, David.

DAVID There are plenty of guys like me and Mike, who'll be glad to show you a good time on your money. Europe is full of bums like me. You'll never be lonesome.

COMFORT But I'd rather have you! Don't you like me, David?

DAVID Yes, I do. But I wouldn't be any fun. You just did something for me, Comfort.

COMFORT What?

DAVID When you hit Mike, you hit me. You hit me hard.

COMFORT I don't know what you mean.

DAVID I've got to get out of your life. (*Quickly*) No, that's not fair. Out of my life, this life. Suddenly it's no life at all.

COMFORT What are you going to do?

DAVID I don't know. I don't know. (*Gently*) Goodbye, Comfort. You'll get along. You know your way around Europe now. You'll get along fine.

(*He touches her nicely, and starts away*)

COMFORT (*Almost desperately*) David, I don't want to be alone.

DAVID (*A moment*) Neither do I.

(*He goes. She looks about, lost and alone. The music of* "Eager Beaver" *sneaks back in, and* COMFORT *cries out*)

COMFORT (*Sings*)

Action! . . . Reaction!
Action! . . . Reaction!

(*And almost as though in answer, the beach boys begin to come on out of the darkness*)

Come, little beaver, I believe a task awaits us,
Each little nibble brings you close to where I am!
Build like a beaver 'till the thing we're building mates us.
Eager beavers always give a . . . "damn!"

(*And now the young men converge on her and surround her, and she reaches up for a moment, but then she is engulfed. Blackout. Almost immediately, the lights come up, and scenery moves into place, and we are in* LUC's *photographic studio in Paris.* LUC *is posing and photographing some models, and* JEANETTE *is dashing about, adjusting lights. The doorbell rings*)

LUC Jeanette, on sonne!

(JEANETTE *goes racing across to answer it*)

JEANETTE Oui, oui, oui, je ne suis pas sourde!

MOLLIE (*Coming on*) It's all right, it's open! Jeanette! Stop!

JEANETTE Allô, Mollie.

MOLLIE Bonjour, chérie. Is Barbara here yet?

JEANETTE Pas encore. Mais toutes les autres.

MOLLIE Oh, yes.

(*She wanders over to inspect the girls*)

LUC She's late again.

MOLLIE Well, she's being awfully gay these days, our Baba. Bonjour, girls.

THE GIRLS (*Brightly, vacantly*) Eh!
(MOLLIE *shudders*)

MOLLIE Well, you don't hire 'em for their minds.

LUC It is finished. Go.

MOLLIE All right, girls, you may close your mouths, now.

LUC C'est fini! Allez, allez!
(*The girls troop off*)

BARBARA (*Off*) I'm here! I made it!

LUC Bravo!
(BARBARA *comes dashing in and kisses* MOLLIE *on the cheek*)

BARBARA Now, Mollie, don't say a word. If you just knew what fun I've been having. We had lunch with the Italian Ambassador, and we couldn't just eat and run. Could we, Marcello. (*She discovers that* MARCELLO *isn't there and starts out again*) Marcello? Where are you? Now, Mollie, be nice; he's awfully shy. Ah, there you are! (*A stocky man in his late thrities appears. He is very well-dressed, not handsome, but rugged and masculine, and very Italian. His head is shiny and bald. He has exaggerated good manners*) May I present Marcello Agnolotti, Mollie Plummer. (*He kisses* MOLLIE'S *hand*) Jeanette Valmy. (*He goes to kiss* JEANETTE'S *hand.* BARBARA *grins at* MOLLIE) He speaks no English and hardly any French. Luc Delbert. (MARCELLO *crosses to shake* LUC'S *hand*) And his father owns most of Milan!

LUC Enchanté, Monsieur.

BARBARA Now we're all friends. Luc, you're waiting for me.

LUC Oh, no!

(BARBARA *and* JEANETTE *start out*)

BARBARA Is the dress pressed?

JEANETTE Oui, c'est ravissant.

BARBARA We'll do a special show for you, Marcello.

(*She and* JEANETTE *go, and* LUC *with them.* MARCELLO *starts to follow*)

MOLLIE No, no, no! Not in there! (*He stops, she smiles, he comes part way back. A moment, and then* MOLLIE *realizes it's up to her, and she speaks up brightly*) Well! I've always wanted to meet someone whose father owned a whole city. (MARCELLO *bows gratefully, knowing only that he is being talked to*) And such a big city, Milan! All those trolley cars. Does your father own the trolley cars? (MARCELLO *bows, smiling*) Good for him. (*She works at her needlepoint*) Do you like Paris? Uh . . . do you . . . like . . . Paree? (*He bows, always smiling*) So do I. But I don't think it's for sale. I like Rome. . . . Roma? (MARCELLO *bows. She looks off into the world with beaming, blissful nostalgia*) Ah, yes! To walk along those beautiful streets, and be pinched by total strangers. (*She smiles over at him*) And I adore Naples. (*He looks puzzled*) Naples? . . . Vesuvius? . . . (*She does a great explosion, and he is delighted. She bows her head in shame, then decides firmly to make one more try*) Siam. How do you feel about Siam? You could be king. (*And that finishes her. The doorbell rings. She calls*) It's open!

BARBARA (*Off*) Mollie?

MOLLIE Yes, dear.

BARBARA (*Off*) How are you and Marcello getting on?

MOLLIE Oh, he's such a babbler, I can't get a word in edgewise.

(BARBARA *sweeps on, in the dress she is to model, and* LUC *and* JEANETTE *follow her*)

BARBARA Oh, Mollie, I love this. (*She parades and twirls to show it off*) Do you like it, Marcello?

(*His mouth drops open in admiration*)

MOLLIE Yes, that's lovely, dear, Up we go. (*She shoos* BARBARA *up onto the platform, and as she passes* MARCELLO, *she smiles companionably at him*) Well! We must talk again, sometime!

LUC Ready?

MOLLIE Wait. Jeanette, the necklace.

(*She takes the necklace out of her bag and starts to put it around* BARBARA's *neck.* JEANETTE *sees* DAVID, *who has entered*)

JEANETTE David!

DAVID (*Quietly*) Hello, Jeanette . . . Luc . . . Mollie . . . (*Pause*)

LUC Uh . . . this is Monsieur . . . uh . . .

(*He appeals to* JEANETTE)

JEANETTE Agnolotti.

LUC Monsieur Agnolotti, David Jordan.

(MARCELLO *offers his hand,* DAVID *shakes it and looks back to* BARBARA)

DAVID I didn't know you were busy, Luc. I just dropped in on the chance . . .

LUC No, we will not be long, David, stay. Or maybe . . . Mollie, I can do this any time. . . .

MOLLIE (*Firmly*) If your guests will excuse us, Luc, I'd like to take some pictures.

BARBARA Mollie . . . please.

MOLLIE If you don't say "no" now, it'll be tougher tomorrow.

BARBARA I have to find that out.

(MOLLIE *shrugs and gives up*)

LUC (*Guiding* MARCELLO *towards her*) Mollie, will you take care of Monsieur Agnolotti?

(MARCELLO *heads straight for* BARBARA *and* MOLLIE *has to head him off, and grab him*)

MOLLIE Oh, no, no, no! (*She takes* MARCELLO *by the arm and starts towards the dressing rooms with him, and calls*) Girls! I have a present for you! (*To* MARCELLO, *as they go off*) Now, they're quite easy to take care of, really . . . (*They are practically gone, and the sentence drifts off*) just one good meal a day, and a sprinkling of diamonds.

(JEANETTE *and* LUC *are gone. Darkness closes in.* DAVID

moves to stand before BARBARA. *They look at each other for a long moment, then she is in his arms)*

BARBARA (*Tearfully*) Crotch-a-mighty!

DAVID You're not up on your bean-water!

BARBARA (*Quavering*) No!

DAVID Bluer'n a whetstone?

BARBARA Oh, much bluer than that!

DAVID (*Holding her close*) No more . . . no more . . .

BARBARA (*Still close to tears*) You went so far away!

DAVID Not far enough. There's no escaping you. There's no getting away from you. (*He sings* "No Strings")

It may be true,
At least it has been said
That the strongest chain in the world
Is a hair from a woman's head.
But I suspect,
For us at least,
The strongest cord of all
Is nothing, but nothing, at all.

(*Refrain*)
No strings—no strings
Except our own devotion;
No other bonds at all.
Let the little folk who need the help
Depend upon vows and such;
We are much too tall.
No ties—no ties
Except our own emotion.

We'll hear some silent call.
If marriage comes we'll let it come
As one of those perfect things
With no strings at all.

(BARBARA *smiles at him, and picks up with the music, and sings her chorus of* "No Strings." *The music continues*)

May I walk you home? I've something to tell you.

BARBARA It's a long walk, home.

DAVID It's a nice day.

BARBARA Like the day we met. (*He nods*) I'll go change. (*She walks off into darkness. He watches her go. And it is, now, very much as it was the day they met. We have almost a sense of going backwards. The music has continued, and David picks up with it and sings part of another chorus of* "No Strings")

DAVID (*Sings*)

Let the little folk who need the help
Depend upon vows and such;
We are much too tall.
No ties—no ties
Except our own emotion.
We'll hear some silent call.
If marriage comes we'll let it come
As one of those perfect things
With no strings at all.

(*During this the scene changes. Scenery is moved, figures wander through, and we are on a Paris street, just as we were on the first day they walked home to-*

gether. BARBARA *appears, changed into street clothes. She wears the same costume she wore in the Prologue.* DAVID *reaches the end of the song, and* BARBARA *sings the tag with him)*

DAVID *and* BARBARA *(Singing)*

A perfect package with no strings at all.

(They smile at each other. A Musician wanders across the stage)

BARBARA You wanted to walk.

DAVID The same place? In the shadow of the Eiffel Tower?

BARBARA Nothing's changed.

DAVID Oh, yes, everything. *(She looks at him curiously)* Let's go.

(They start to walk. The Musician wanders past them and off)

BARBARA What did you mean, everything's changed?

DAVID Well, let's say that I've changed. Would you settle for that? *(She stops to face him)* Yes. I've stopped running. I'm going to work.

BARBARA Oh, David!

DAVID And now I've something to ask you. How would you like to go live in the South of France?

BARBARA And work!

DAVID It's a wonderful house on Cap Ferrat. Very small but right on the sea. Actually, it's the guest house of a friend of mine, Mario Russo, the Italian movie producer. He's a good one; he does good things.

BARBARA And he offered you this house.

DAVID More than that. He offered me a job.

BARBARA (*Suddenly afraid*) A job!

DAVID I bumped into him on the train coming back to Paris. As soon as he saw me, he grabbed me. And the money's not bad, not bad at all. He's got a good script, but he wants me to stay with the picture all through the shooting and write the additional dialogue.

BARBARA (*In a panic*) David! They don't give Pulitzer Prizes for additional dialogue!

DAVID (*Pressing hard*) Don't you see? It's a way to make money! To buy time!

BARBARA For what?

DAVID To do what I want to do! Write!

BARBARA Where? Here? In Paris? Or in the South of France? Or in Biarritz? Where all your charming friends can find you? You're fooling yourself!

DAVID I can do it with you.

BARBARA (*Close to tears*) No. You'll fall into the trap again. Your friends will turn up and you'll be seduced again.

Devoured again. And I won't be able to save you. Oh, David!

DAVID Then what? What?

(A long moment, as she stares at him, trying hard to find the thing to say. And then the tears begin to come, and she turns away sharply not to show them. Finally she gathers herself and turns back to him, composed)

BARBARA Go home. *(He turns and looks at her. She sings)*

Let the snow come down
Before the sun comes up.
Maine is the main thing.
Let the lake and hills
Become a frozen cup.
Twenty below in Maine.
Get the sleigh, turn about.
That's a nice team.
Make believe all of it's yours.
Take a breath, blow it out,
No, it ain't steam.
It'll be warmer indoors.

DAVID *and* BARBARA *(Sing)*

Let the snow come down
Before it starts to rain.
Under the covers—it's cozy.

DAVID

Far away, cross the bay
Goes an old train:
Woo-hoo, woo-hoo.

(Sound of train)

BARBARA

Woo-hoo, woo-hoo.

(*Sound of train*)

DAVID

Mainly I do like Maine.

(*Pause*)

DAVID There's a little house way out by the quarry that's been abandoned for years. I can fix it up myself. I'm very handy with a hammer.

BARBARA David, you're going . . .

DAVID (*Smiling*) Home.

BARBARA To work.

DAVID Really work. The kind of work I haven't done for too many years.

BARBARA Ah, David.

DAVID And you will finally get to see your hackmatack trees. And the lobster boats with their spankers out on Jericho Bay.

(*That is not what she expected, and it is almost as though her heart had stopped*)

BARBARA (*After a moment, expressionless*) You want me to go with you.

DAVID Of course. I can't go without you.

BARBARA Back to America.

DAVID Yes.

BARBARA (*Gently*) What would I do there?

DAVID You'd be my wife.

BARBARA David, I'm afraid.

DAVID No, don't be.

BARBARA (*Turning on him, appealing*) But this is my home! My safe and beautiful world! Can I leave it for yours?

DAVID Yes.

BARBARA (*Suddenly in his arms*) I'm afraid.

DAVID (*Strongly*) I won't go without you!

(*A pause, and then she looks up at him and smiles reassuringly*)

BARBARA (*Lightly*) But of course I'll go. I have to go. I'm your wife. (*She kisses him lightly. He stares at her searchingly*) Will we go soon?

DAVID As soon as we can.

BARBARA You'll have to tell me what to pack. I don't think I have the clothes for a rugged, coast-of-Maine woman.

DAVID (*Smiling*) You can get them at the general store.

BARBARA But I would like to take all my beautiful Paris dresses! May I?

DAVID (*Smiling*) You won't have much use for 'em there.

BARBARA (*Gaily*) Oh, I can wear them to the Saturday-night dances! (*A moment*) Don't they have Saturday-night dances?

DAVID (*Quietly*) Yes, quite often.

BARBARA (*With a small smile of irony*) But we won't go.

DAVID (*Almost roughly*) Of course we'll go!

BARBARA Once. To show we're not cowards. (*Then, with a bright smile*) Well, the hell with the dresses! I'll give them away! Oh, no, I'll sell them! We need the money!

DAVID Look, Barbara, it's not going to be easy, we both know that—

BARBARA (*Brightly*) Of course we know it! We're neither one of us fools. It won't be like Paris!

DAVID (*Grimly*) No. No one's going to ask you to dinner at Maxim's. You'll be alone a lot of the time. I'll be working.

BARBARA Oh, I'll read, and I'll sew. I might even join the ladies' sewing circle. (*And then*) No. (*She smiles*) Well, anyway, I can go for long walks through the woods and along the shore.

DAVID (*Turns away, tormented*) Ah, what a damned foolish thing it is.

BARBARA What?

DAVID That your warm, lovely world should be so bad for me, and the world I'm going back to so impossible for you.

BARBARA David, I'm going with you.

DAVID No, you're not.

BARBARA David!

DAVID No, I won't let you. This is your home. You're going to stay here, where you belong. (*She looks down dully, lost. He takes her in his arms*) I'll be back, I promise. When I've done what I have to do; found a way to work again. Nothing could keep me from you. Will you wait?

BARBARA (*She leans back and looks at him pathetically*) And what'll I do until then?

DAVID You'll go on as you are . . .

BARBARA And at night? Alone? Then? (*She holds him tight*) How do I live without you?

DAVID Only one way. To say to ourselves that this never happened. It was all in our minds. You are something that hasn't happened to me, yet. It's the only way I'll be able to live. Do you understand that? Can you say it? We never met.

BARBARA We never met.

DAVID We have yet to meet.

BARBARA We have yet to meet.

(*The music enters as it did at the beginning of the play, and they sing* "The Sweetest Sounds")

DAVID *and* BARBARA (*Sing*)

The sweetest sounds I'll ever hear
Are still inside my head.
The kindest words I'll ever know
Are waiting to be said.
The most entrancing sight of all
Is yet for me to see.
And the dearest love in all the world
Is waiting somewhere for me.
Is waiting somewhere, somewhere for me.

(*Darkness closes in. The two Musicians we first saw—the flute and the clarinet—wander on, playing, and drift off into darkness.* BARBARA *and* DAVID *stand alone in their separate lights, singing, already in their separate worlds, and as they come to the final phrases of the song, they move and pass each other, unseeing, unaware, and walk into darkness*)

Curtain